Contents

Grade 2 Standards—Reading: Informational Text

A. Key Ideas and Details	
	1. Ask and answer such questions as *who, what, where, when, why,* and *how* to demonstrate understanding of key details in a text.
	2. Identify the main topic of a multiparagraph text as well as the focus of specific paragraphs within the text.
	3. Describe the connection between a series of historical events, scientific ideas or concepts, or steps in technical procedures in a text.
B. Craft and Structure	
	1. Determine the meaning of words and phrases in a text relevant to a *grade 2 topic or subject area.*
	2. Know and use various text features (e.g., captions, bold print, subheadings, glossaries, indexes, electronic menus, icons) to locate key facts or information in a text efficiently.
	3. Identify the main purpose of a text, including what the author wants to answer, explain, or describe.
C. Integration of Knowledge and Ideas	
	1. Explain how specific images (e.g., a diagram showing how a machine works) contribute to and clarify a text.
	2. Describe how reasons support specific points the author makes in a text.
	3. Compare and contrast the most important points presented by two texts on the same topic.
D. Range of Reading and Level of Text Complexity	
	1. By the end of year, read and comprehend informational texts, including history/social studies, science, and technical texts, in the grades 2–3 text complexity band proficiently, with scaffolding as needed at the high end of the range.

Visit www.creativeteaching.com to find out how this book correlates to Common Core and/or State Standards.

Reading Passages Specific Standards

Text	A. 1	A. 2	A. 3	B. 1	B. 2	B. 3	C. 1	C. 2	C. 3	D. 1
A Trip to a Farm (p. 6)	✔						✔		✔	✔
All About Birds (p. 9)	✔	✔	✔			✔	✔			✔
Dragonflies (p. 11)	✔		✔		✔		✔			✔
Big and Blue (p. 13)	✔			✔			✔			✔
Squirrel Adaptations (p. 15)	✔	✔	✔		✔					✔
Life Cycle of a Brown Bear (p. 17)	✔			✔	✔					✔
Life Cycle of a Monarch Butterfly (p. 19)	✔		✔	✔			✔			✔
Three Types of Ice (p. 21)	✔	✔			✔	✔				✔
Freezing Rain (p. 23)	✔	✔	✔				✔			✔
Fog (p. 25)	✔		✔					✔		✔
Snow Globes (p. 27)	✔		✔	✔						✔
How We Use Water at Home (p. 29)	✔							✔		✔
Wind Makes Things Move (p. 31)	✔		✔	✔	✔					✔
How Do We Use Air? (p. 33)	✔	✔	✔							✔
Drying Clothes (p. 35)	✔		✔					✔		✔
Sliding and Rolling (p. 37)	✔		✔							✔
Things That Spin (p. 39)	✔		✔	✔						✔
Things with Wheels (p. 41)	✔				✔		✔			✔
Moving in a Wheelchair (p. 43)	✔	✔				✔	✔	✔		✔
Be Active Every Day (p. 45)	✔		✔		✔		✔			✔
Your Body Needs Water (p. 48)	✔		✔							✔
Finding New Friends (p. 50)	✔		✔		✔	✔				✔
Teasing (p. 53)	✔		✔	✔	✔					✔
When You Are Sick (p. 55)	✔		✔			✔				✔
Stay Safe in the Sun (p. 57)	✔		✔			✔	✔			✔
Birthday Traditions (p. 59)	✔		✔	✔						✔
A Birthday in Mexico (p. 61)	✔		✔		✔		✔			✔
Christmas (p. 63)	✔						✔			✔
Hanukkah (p. 65)	✔						✔			✔
Diwali (p. 67)	✔						✔	✔		✔
Eid al-Fitr (p. 69)	✔									✔
The Tricky Turtle (p. 71)	✔									✔
The Grasshopper and the Ant (p. 73)	✔							✔		✔
The Lion and the Mouse (p. 75)	✔									✔
The Rooster and the Sun (p. 77)	✔									✔
How Communities Change (p. 79)	✔				✔			✔		✔
People on the Move (p. 81)	✔	✔								✔
Hospitals and Community Centers (p. 83)	✔	✔			✔		✔			✔
What Does a School Custodian Do? (p. 86)	✔						✔			✔
What Does a School Librarian Do? (p. 88)	✔	✔						✔		✔
What Does a Crossing Guard Do? (p. 90)	✔				✔		✔	✔		✔
What Is the Internet? (p. 92)	✔				✔					✔
Convincing People to Buy a Product (p. 94)	✔			✔						✔
The Wright Brothers (p. 97)	✔		✔		✔	✔	✔			✔
Helen Keller (p. 99)	✔	✔			✔			✔		✔

Introduction

Reading comprehension is the cornerstone of a child's academic success. By completing the activities in this book, children will develop and reinforce essential reading comprehension skills. Children will benefit from a wide variety of opportunities to practice engaging with text as active readers who can self-monitor their understanding of what they have read.

Children will focus on the following:

Identifying the Purpose of the Text
- The reader understands, and can tell you, why they read the text.

Understanding the Text
- What is the main idea of the text?
- What are the supporting details?
- Which parts are facts and which parts are opinions?

Analyzing the Text
- How does the reader's background knowledge enhance the text clues to help the reader answer questions about the text or draw conclusions?
- What inferences can be made by using information from the text with what the reader already knows?
- How does the information from the text help the reader make predictions?
- What is the cause and effect between events?

Making Connections
How does the topic or information they are reading remind the reader about what they already know?
- Text-to-self connections: How does this text relate to your own life?
- Text-to-text connections: Have I read something like this before? How is this text similar to something I have read before? How is this text different from something I have read before?
- Text-to-world connections: What does this text remind you of in the real world?

Using Text Features
- How do different text features help the reader?

Text Features

Text features help the reader to understand the text better. Here is a list of text features with a brief explanation on how they help the reader.

Contents	Here the reader will find the title of each section, what page each text starts on within sections, and where to find specific information.
Chapter Title	The chapter title gives the reader an idea of what the text will be about. The chapter title is often followed by subheadings within the text.
Title and Subheading	The title or topic is found at the top of the page. The subheading is right above a paragraph. There may be more than one subheading in a text.
Map	Maps help the reader understand where something is happening. It is a visual representation of a location.
Diagram and Illustration	Diagrams and illustrations give the reader additional visual information about the text.
Label	A label tells the reader the title of a map, diagram, or illustration. Labels also draw attention to specific elements within a visual.
Caption	Captions are words that are placed underneath the visuals. Captions give the reader more information about the map, diagram, or illustration.
Fact Box	A fact box tells the reader extra information about the topic.
Table	A table presents text information in columns and rows in a concise and often comparative way.
Bold and Italic text	**Bold** and *italic* text are used to emphasize a word or words, and signify that this is important vocabulary.

A Trip to a Farm

Lily and Sandro wrote about their class trip to a farm.

Our Class Trip—by Lily

We went to a farm. We saw lots of animals. We saw chickens and sheep and cows.

We saw pigs. There were little baby pigs. They were cute. They have pink noses. Pigs have flat noses.

Baby pig

We saw corn growing. The corn was not very tall. The corn has to grow tall. Then it grows the part you can eat.

Chicks are baby chickens. The chicks are yellow and fluffy. I got to hold a chick. That was the best part of the trip.

Our Trip to a Farm—by Sandro

We went on a trip to a farm. Mr. Crane is the farmer.

The farm has different animals. We fed the pigs. We saw Mr. Crane milk a cow. We saw sheep, too.

The farm has chickens. The chickens lay eggs. Baby chicks come out of the eggs.

Mr. Crane has a **tractor**. It has big wheels and small wheels.

Farm tractor

Mr. Crane let me sit on the tractor. That was the most fun of all.

"A Trip to a Farm"—Think About It

1. Who wrote about each thing? Circle the correct answer. The first one is done for you.

sheep	Lily	Sandro	⟨Lily and Sandro⟩
Mr. Crane	Lily	Sandro	Lily and Sandro
baby pigs	Lily	Sandro	Lily and Sandro
chicken eggs	Lily	Sandro	Lily and Sandro
chicks	Lily	Sandro	Lily and Sandro
corn	Lily	Sandro	Lily and Sandro
tractor	Lily	Sandro	Lily and Sandro

2. Sandro said the tractor has big wheels and small wheels. Are the small wheels at the front or the back of the tractor? Tell how you know.

_____

_____

_____

_____

3. Tell which part of the trip Lily and Sandro each liked best.

_____

_____

_____

_____

"A Trip to a Farm"—Think About It (continued)

4. What does the text remind you of?

5. If you could have a farm, what type of farm would it be?
Explain your thinking.

Draw a picture of your farm.

All About Birds

There are many different types of birds. A **robin**, an **ostrich**, and a **penguin** are all birds. How are all birds the same?

Robin

1. All birds have feathers. Feathers help birds stay dry and warm. Feathers also help birds fly.

2. All birds have wings. The wings are covered with **feathers**. Most birds use their wings to fly. Not all birds can fly. A penguin and an ostrich have wings, but these birds cannot fly.

3. All birds lay eggs. Birds sit on their eggs to keep them warm. A baby bird grows inside each egg. If an egg gets cold, the baby bird growing inside the egg might die.

4. All birds have ear holes, but no ears. You cannot see the ear holes because they are covered with feathers.

5. All birds are **warm-blooded**. A bird's body makes its own heat. Feathers help keep the heat inside the bird's body.

6. All birds have two legs. You will never see a bird that has more than two legs.

7. No birds have teeth. Birds have hard beaks that they use to eat.

A penguin with an egg.

Ostrich

"All About Birds"—Think About It

1. This text answers a question about birds. What is the question?

_____

_____

2. How do feathers help birds stay warm?

_____

_____

3. People are warm-blooded, just like birds. What do people use to help their bodies stay warm?

_____

_____

_____

4. What part of your body does the same thing as a bird's beak?

_____

_____

5. Why do birds need to keep their eggs warm?

_____

_____

6. Tell one new thing you learned about an ostrich by looking at the picture.

_____

_____

_____

Dragonflies

What Do Dragonflies Look Like?

A dragonfly has a long body and big wings. Many dragonflies have wings that you can see through. Dragonflies can be different colors.

What Do Dragonflies Eat?

Mosquitoes and flies are two insects that dragonflies eat. Sometimes, a large dragonfly will eat a smaller dragonfly.

How Do Dragonflies Hunt?

Dragonflies use their large eyes to find an insect to eat. They make a basket shape with their legs and trap the insect inside. Next, they bite the insect so it does not get away. Then they find a place to eat it.

How Do Dragonflies Grow?

An adult dragonfly lays eggs in water where plants grow. The baby that comes out of each egg is called a **nymph** (say it like this: *nimf*). The nymph does not have wings. It lives in the water.

When the nymph is big enough, it crawls up the stem of a plant to get out of the water. Then the nymph **sheds** its skin. An adult dragonfly with wings comes out of the old skin.

Life Cycle of a Dragonfly

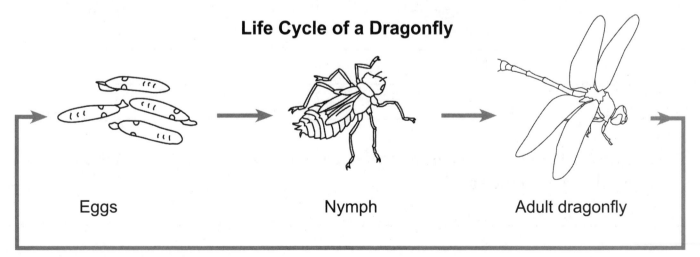

| Eggs | Nymph | Adult dragonfly |

"Dragonflies"—Think About It

1. How many wings does a dragonfly have? Tell where you found the answer.

_____

_____

2. What kind of sentence is each of the subheadings in this text? Tell how you know.

_____

_____

3. Tell how a dragonfly uses the body part below to help it hunt.

Large eyes: _____

_____

Legs: _____

_____

Mouth: _____

_____

4. Why do dragonflies lay eggs in water that has plants growing out of it?

_____

_____

_____

5. Why does the life cycle diagram have an arrow that goes from the adult dragonfly back to the eggs?

_____

_____

Big and Blue

What is the biggest animal on Earth? This animal is even bigger than a dinosaur. Can you guess the animal? It is a blue whale.

Baby Blue Whales

A baby blue whale has just come out of its mother's body. The **newborn** whale weighs as much as an adult elephant. The baby drinks lots of milk from the mother. Baby blue whales grow quickly.

Adult Blue Whales

Everything about an adult blue whale is big. The whale's body is as long as three school buses. The whale's tongue is so big that 50 people could stand on it. The whale's heart is as big as a small car. Your heart is as big as your fist.

Blue Whales Breathe Air

Whales are mammals. All mammals breathe air into their lungs. A blue whale breathes through two holes on top of its head. These holes are called **blowholes**. They are close together, like your nostrils.

The whale swims to the surface of the water to breathe. The top of the whale's head sticks out of the water. The whale blows old air out of the blowholes. Then it sucks **fresh** air into the blowholes.

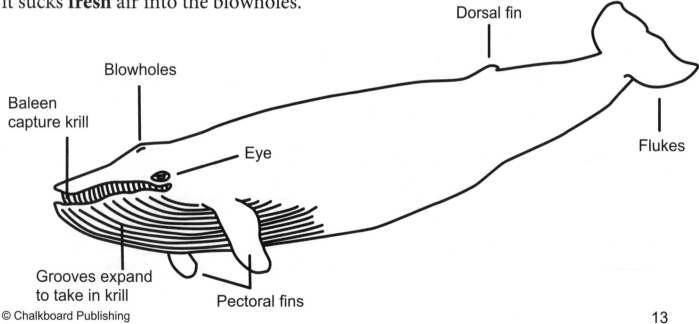

© Chalkboard Publishing

"Big and Blue"—Think About It

1. When is a baby whale a newborn whale?

_____

_____

2. What food helps a baby blue whale grow quickly?

_____

_____

3. The text says that blowholes are close together, like your nostrils. Tell another way that blowholes and your nostrils are the same. (Hint: Think about what blowholes and nostrils do.)

_____

_____

4. Complete the sentences to show how a blue whale compares to other things. Put a period at the end of each sentence.

A blue whale is bigger than _____

A newborn blue whale weighs as much as _____

_____

An adult blue whale has a body that is as long as _____

_____

5. How many fins does a blue whale have? Tell how you know.

_____

_____

_____

Squirrel Adaptations

Squirrels have adaptations to help them survive.

What Is an Adaptation?

An **adaptation** is something that helps an animal survive. There are two types of adaptions. Some adaptations are body parts. Other adaptations are things the animal does.

Squirrel Body Parts

Squirrels have strong teeth. Squirrels like to eat nuts. Nuts have a hard shell on the outside. Squirrels use their teeth to break open the shell on a nut. Strong teeth are an adaptation.

Squirrels have sharp claws. Sharp claws help squirrels climb trees. Sharp claws also help squirrels hold on to nuts when they are eating. Sharp claws are an adaptation.

Things a Squirrel Does

Squirrels bury nuts. Squirrels dig up the nuts when it is hard to find food. Burying nuts to eat later is an adaptation.

Squirrels climb trees. Climbing up a tall tree is how squirrels get away from danger. Climbing trees is an adaptation.

Squirrels make noises when danger is near. The noises tell other squirrels that danger is near. Making noises to warn of danger is an adaptation.

Squirrels gather acorns.

"Squirrel Adaptations"—Think About It

1. What do adaptations help all animals do?

_____

_____

2. What are the two types of adaptations?

_____

_____

_____

3. Which subheading would you look under to find out about a squirrel's teeth?

_____

4. What is the last paragraph about? Write your answer in one sentence.

_____

_____

5. How does burying nuts help squirrels survive?

_____

_____

6. Which adaptation does a squirrel use to help other squirrels? Tell how this
   adaptation helps other squirrels.

_____

_____

_____

Life Cycle of a Brown Bear

Hibernating in a Den

Winter is coming. A female brown bear finds a cave or digs a cave in dirt. The cave will be her **den**. She **hibernates** in the den during the winter. Hibernating is like sleeping all winter long.

A Cub Is Born

A baby brown bear is growing inside its mother's body. The baby bear is born while the mother is hibernating in the den. The baby bear is called a cub. The cub drinks milk from its mother's body. The cub grows bigger.

Mother bear and her cub

Leaving the Den

The mother bear stops hibernating when spring comes. The mother bear and the cub come out of the den. The cub learns by watching its mother. The cub learns how to find food.

The cub eats lots of food to help it grow. The cub stays with its mother until it is two or three years old. Then it is time for the cub to go away to live on its own.

The Cub Becomes an Adult

The cub becomes an adult bear when it is five or six years old. At age 5 or 6, a female brown bear is old enough to find a **mate**. Then she will have her own cub when she hibernates in winter.

"Life Cycle of a Brown Bear"—Think About It

1. What is a den?

_____

_____

_____

2. When does a brown bear hibernate?

_____

_____

3. The cub needs food to grow after it is born. What is the cub's first food?

_____

_____

4. What does a mother bear teach her cub?

_____

_____

_____

5. How many years does the cub stay with its mother?

_____

_____

6. This text has four types of text features. Three types of text features are in bold print. Name the four types of text features.

_____

_____

_____

Life Cycle of a Monarch Butterfly

Find out what happens in the life of a monarch butterfly.

Eggs

A monarch butterfly lays tiny eggs on the leaves of a milkweed plant. The eggs stay there for a few days until it is the right time to **hatch**.

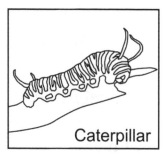

Eggs

Caterpillar

An egg hatches and out comes a tiny caterpillar. The caterpillar eats milkweed leaves to grow bigger. Soon the caterpillar is too big for its skin. The caterpillar sheds its old skin. The new skin underneath is bigger. The caterpillar keeps eating and shedding its skin as it grows.

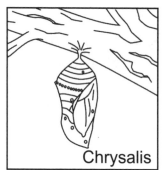

Caterpillar

Chrysalis

The caterpillar hangs from a branch, then makes a **chrysalis** (say it like this: *kris-a-lis*). Inside, the caterpillar turns into a butterfly.

Chrysalis

Butterfly

After about nine days, a monarch butterfly breaks out of the chrysalis. The butterfly flies around and lands on flowers. The butterfly eats nectar. Nectar is a sweet liquid inside flowers. Soon the monarch butterfly will be ready to lay eggs.

Adult butterfly

Fun Facts
- Monarch butterflies are easy to spot because of their bold orange, black, and white markings.
- Monarch butterflies use their antennae to smell things.

"Life Cycle of a Monarch Butterfly"—Think About It

1. Write a number beside each sentence to show the order things happen in the life of a monarch butterfly.

    _____ The caterpillar hangs from a branch and makes a chrysalis.

    _____ A caterpillar comes out of an egg.

    _____ The monarch butterfly eats nectar.

    _____ The caterpillar eats leaves to grow.

    _____ A monarch butterfly comes out of the chrysalis.

    _____ The caterpillar sheds its skin as it grows.

2. The caterpillar sheds its old skin. What does *sheds* mean?

    ☐ makes   ☐ gets rid of   ☐ hangs   ☐ flies away

3. Why is a milkweed plant a good place for monarch butterflies to lay eggs? Look for a clue in the text.

    _____

    _____

4. How do you know that the caterpillars eat lots of milkweed leaves?

    _____

    _____

5. Compare the caterpillar's legs and the monarch butterfly's legs. Tell two differences you see.

    _____

    _____

    _____

    _____

Three Types of Ice

What different types of ice do we see in nature?

Snow

Did you know that snowflakes are tiny pieces of ice? **Water vapor** in very cold air **freezes** into snowflakes. Snowflakes have different shapes. Many snowflakes are shaped like a star.

A snowflake

Frost

Frost is ice you see on the outside of windows. Sometimes you can see frost on plant leaves. Where does the frost come from?

Frost starts as water vapor in the air. The water vapor freezes on a window or leaf that is very cold. People scrape frost off car windows in winter. Frost makes it hard to see out a window.

Hail

Hail is balls of ice that fall from the sky. Each ball of ice is called a hailstone. Most of the time, hailstones are the size of a pea or smaller. Sometimes hailstones are much bigger.

A hailstone starts as a tiny drop of water in the air. The drop of water freezes into a tiny piece of ice. Moving air pushes the tiny piece of ice into drops of water in the air. The water drops freeze on the piece of ice and make it bigger. Soon a hailstone becomes heavy and falls to the ground.

A small hailstone and a big hailstone.

"Three Types of Ice"—Think About It

1. The author wrote this text to answer a question. What is the question?

_____

_____

_____

There are six paragraphs in the text. Number the paragraphs from 1 to 6. Then use the numbers to answer the questions in this box.

2. Which paragraph talks about the different sizes hailstones can be?

_____

3. Which paragraph tells why people need to scrape frost off car windows?

_____

4. Which paragraph tells about the shapes of snowflakes?

_____

5. Which paragraph tells you about how hailstones are made?

_____

6. Which paragraph asks a question about frost?

_____

---

7. The text has three subheadings in bold print. Tell how a reader could use the subheadings to find the answer to each question in the box above.

_____

_____

_____

_____

Freezing Rain

Rain falls from the sky. Sometimes the air close to the ground is very cold. When rain hits the ground, it freezes into ice. Rain that freezes is called freezing rain.

Freezing rain makes ice on roads. Icy roads can be dangerous. Cars can slip and slide. Cars might have trouble stopping. Ice on roads can make cars crash into each other.

Freezing rain makes ice on sidewalks. People can slip and slide on an icy sidewalk. Sometimes people fall and get hurt.

Sand makes ice less **slippery**. People put sand on icy roads and sidewalks. Sand helps to keep people and cars from slipping and sliding.

Ice on sidewalks can make people fall.

Salt makes ice melt. People put salt on icy roads and sidewalks to melt the ice.

Freezing rain makes ice on trees. Ice makes tree branches heavy. Lots of ice can make a tree branch break and fall. Falling branches can be dangerous. They can hurt people. Falling branches can also damage cars and houses.

Sometimes freezing rain makes ice on outdoor skating rinks. That makes skaters happy. Skaters need slippery ice to skate on.

Ice on trees can make branches break.

"Freezing Rain"—Think About It

1. Water freezes when it gets very cold. What makes rain get so cold it freezes?

_____

_____

2. Finish the sentence to tell what the second paragraph is about.

The second paragraph is about what can happen when

_____

3. How does putting sand on icy sidewalks help people?

_____

_____

_____

4. What happens when people put salt on ice?

_____

_____

5. Look at the pictures. Tell one way that a falling branch can damage a car.

_____

_____

_____

6. People do not put sand on the ice at a skating rink. Tell why.

_____

_____

_____

Fog

What Is Fog?

Fog is made of many tiny drops of water. The drops of water float in the air. The drops can float in air because they are so tiny.

Clouds are also made of tiny drops of water in the air. Fog is like a cloud that is close to the ground.

Fog makes it hard to see far. Very thick fog can make it hard to see things that are close to you.

Why Can Fog Be Dangerous to People?

Fog can be dangerous if you are crossing a street. You might not see a car coming. The driver of a car might not be able to see you. Be very careful crossing a street when it is foggy.

Why Can Fog Be Dangerous to Boats?

Fog can be thick over a lake or ocean. People in a boat can get lost if they cannot see the land. Some places have **lighthouses** to help people in boats.

A lighthouse is a tall tower with a big, bright light at the top. The light shines out over the water. People in boats can see the bright light when it is foggy. The light helps to keep boats from getting lost.

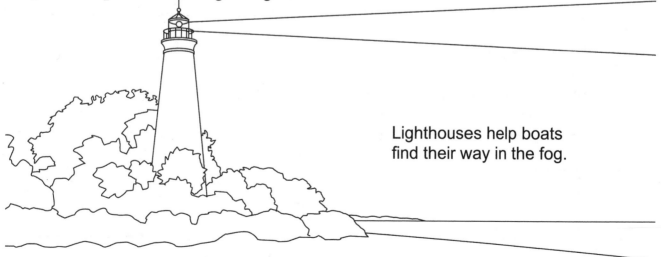

Lighthouses help boats find their way in the fog.

"Fog"—Think About It

1. How are fog and clouds the same?

_____

_____

_____

_____

2. What is one way that a cloud and fog are different?

_____

_____

3. The text says that fog can be dangerous to people crossing a street. Give two reasons why.

First reason:_____

_____

Second reason:_____

_____

4. Why might people in a boat get lost when there is thick fog?

_____

_____

5. Why are lighthouses always near a lake or an ocean?

_____

_____

_____

_____

Snow Globes

Have you ever seen a snow globe? A snow globe is made of **solids** and a **liquid**.

The Outside of a Snow Globe

A snow globe has a clear ball made of plastic. The ball is called the **globe**. The globe is hollow. The globe sits on a piece of wood or plastic called the **base**. Wood and plastic are solids.

Inside a Snow Globe

Different snow globes have different objects inside. You might see buildings, trees, animals, or people. The snow globe on this page has a snowman inside. The objects in a snow globe are made of plastic. The plastic objects are solids.

Snowman in a snow globe

There are small flakes of snow in a snow globe. The snowflakes are not real snow made of frozen water. The snowflakes in a snow globe are made of plastic. The snowflakes are solids.

A snow globe has water inside. The water is a liquid.

How to Make It Snow in a Snow Globe

You shake the snow globe to make the water start moving. The moving water pushes on the snowflakes. Then the snowflakes start moving around inside the globe. Soon the snowflakes start to fall to the bottom of the globe. It is snowing in the snow globe!

"Snow Globes"—Think About It

1. *Globe* is a name for a shape. What shape is a globe?

_____

_____

2. What parts of a snow globe are solids?

_____

_____

3. Why does the globe on a snow globe need to be hollow?

_____

_____

_____

4. How is real snow different from the snow in a snow globe?

_____

_____

_____

5. Where is the snow in the globe before someone shakes the snow globe?

_____

_____

6. Someone shakes a snow globe. Why do the snowflakes start moving around inside the globe?

_____

_____

_____

How We Use Water at Home

Read about different ways we use water at home.

Water for Drinking

Living things need water. We drink water when we are **thirsty**. People give water to their pets. Animals need water, too.

Water for Cooking

We use water to cook. People use water to make soup. People use water to cook eggs. Eggs cook in **boiling** water. Boiling water is very hot. Stay away from boiling water.

Pets need water to drink.

Water for Plants

Plants are living things, so plants need water. People water plants in their homes. People water plants in gardens. Garden plants also get water when it rains.

Water for Washing

Water helps make things clean. People use water to take a bath or shower. People also use water when they wash their hands.

Indoor plants need people to water them.

People use water to wash clothes. They use water to wash cars and mop floors. Water helps make dirty dishes clean again.

"How We Use Water at Home"—Think About It

1. Name three living things in the text.

_____

_____

_____

2. What is one reason why people drink water?

_____

_____

3. Why can boiling water hurt you?

_____

_____

4. The text tells two ways people use water outside. What are the two ways?

_____

_____

5. How does water help us after we cook and eat?

_____

_____

6. Hamid was going to water his garden. He looked outside. The dirt in the garden was wet. "I do not need to water my garden today," he said. How did the plants in Hamid's garden probably get water?

_____

_____

Wind Makes Things Move

Wind is air that is moving. Moving air **pushes** on things. That is how wind makes things move. You cannot see wind, but you can see when wind makes things move.

Wind Makes Trees Move

Wind makes tree branches move. The branches move back and forth. The leaves move in the wind. Wind can blow leaves off trees. Then the wind blows the leaves through the air.

Wind blows leaves off trees.

Wind Makes Flags Move

A flag flies when wind makes it move. Moving air pushes on the flag. The flag hangs down when there is no wind.

Wind Makes Kites Fly

You need wind to fly a kite. The wind pushes the kite up into the air. The kite is on a string. You need to hold on tight to the string. The wind will blow your kite away if you let go of the string.

Wind Makes Clouds Move

A cloud moves across the sky. What makes the cloud move? Wind is pushing on the cloud. Strong wind makes clouds move quickly. Clouds move slowly when the wind is not strong.

Wind helps people fly kites.

"Wind Makes Things Move"—Think About It

1. What is wind?

_____

_____

_____

2. How does wind make things move?

_____

_____

3. Which subheading would you look under to find out about how wind makes leaves move?

_____

_____

4. Why does a flag hang down when the wind stops?

_____

_____

5. Why does a kite need to have a string to hold?

_____

_____

6. Kim watched a cloud move across the sky. The cloud started moving faster. Why did the cloud start moving faster?

_____

_____

_____

How Do We Use Air?

Read about some different ways people use air.

Breathing

People need air to **breathe**. We breathe in to pull air down into our lungs. We push the air out of our **lungs** when we breathe out. We breathe fast when we run. Our body needs more air when we run.

Filling Tires

Bike tires and car tires are filled with air. People use a pump to push air inside tires. A tire gets flat when it has a hole in it. The air inside the tire goes out the hole. People glue a patch on the hole to cover it. Then they use a pump to fill the tire with air again.

People use a pump to push air inside bicycle tires.

Drying Hair

People use a hair dryer to dry their hair. The hair dryer sucks in cool air. Next, the hair dryer heats the air to make it warm. Then the hair dryer blows out warm air. Warm moving air makes hair dry quickly.

Gathering Leaves

Some people use a leaf blower to gather leaves. A leaf blower blows out air that pushes leaves. People use a leaf blower to push all the leaves to one spot. Then they put the leaves in garbage bags.

Leaf blowers use air to push leaves into one spot.

"How Do We Use Air?"—Think About It

1. What is the main topic in this text?

_____

2. How does your breathing change when your body needs more air?

_____

_____

3. Frank's bike got a flat tire. He used a pump to push more air inside the tire. Soon the tire was flat again. Tell why.

_____

_____

_____

4. What is one thing that a leaf blower and a hair dryer both do?

_____

_____

5. How does a leaf blower make leaves move?

_____

_____

6. Answer the riddle about something else that uses air.

I move across a floor.

I pull air inside me.

When I pull air inside, dirt comes, too.

What am I?

_____

Drying Clothes

Clothes are wet when they come out of a washing machine. How do wet clothes get dry?

There is water in wet clothes. If you squeeze the clothes, you will see water come out of them. Clothes get dry when the water in them **evaporates**, or dries up.

It can take a long time for all the water in clothes to evaporate. A clothes dryer makes the water evaporate more quickly.

How a Clothes Dryer Works

A clothes dryer blows air on wet clothes. Moving air makes the water in the clothes evaporate more quickly. The water turns into water **vapor** in the air. The clothes are dry when all the water in them has evaporated.

Moving air makes water evaporate more quickly. Heat also makes water evaporate more quickly. A clothes dryer uses heat and moving air to dry clothes quickly.

A clothes dryer heats the air that it blows on the clothes. The air in the dryer is moving and it is warm. The inside of the dryer spins. Warm air moves around all the clothes as they tumble in the dryer. The warm, moving air makes the water in the clothes evaporate quickly. Soon the clothes are dry.

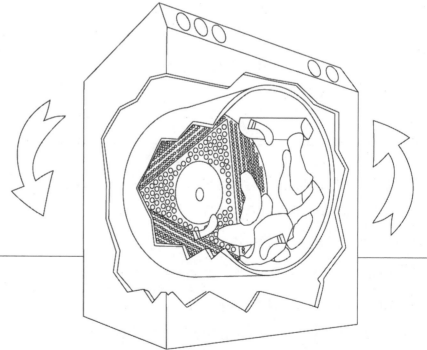

The inside of a clothes dryer spins to make the clothes tumble.

"Drying Clothes"—Think About It

1. Wet clothes feel wet. What is another way you can tell that there is water in wet clothes?

_____

_____

2. When water evaporates, what does it turn into?

_____

_____

3. Give two reasons why a clothes dryer dries clothes quickly.

Reason 1: _____

_____

Reason 2: _____

_____

4. Why do the clothes in a clothes dryer tumble?

_____

_____

5. When will clothes hanging on a clothesline dry fastest? Mark an X in the box beside the correct answer.

☐ On a cool, windy day.

☐ On a warm day.

☐ On a warm, windy day.

Tell why you think the answer you chose is correct.

_____

_____

Sliding and Rolling

Sliding

Emma is playing hockey. She shoots the puck. The puck moves across the ice. How is the puck moving? The puck is **sliding**.

An object slides when it moves across a **surface** and is always touching the surface. A puck moves across the ice. The ice is a surface. The puck is always touching the ice as it moves.

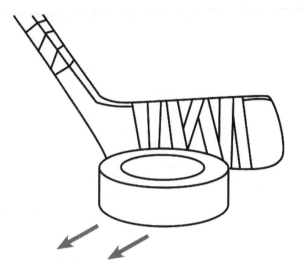

Hockey pucks slide across ice.

Rolling

Kenji is playing with marbles. He shoots a marble across the floor. The floor is a surface. The marble moves across a surface. The marble is always touching the surface of the floor. Is the marble sliding?

The marble is not sliding. The marble is **rolling**. An object rolls when it turns around and around as it moves across a surface. An object that is sliding does not turn around and around as it moves.

Marbles roll across the floor.

Comparing Rolling and Sliding

A sliding object moves across a surface. A rolling object also moves across a surface.

A sliding object is always touching a surface. A rolling object is also always touching a surface.

A sliding object does not turn around and around as it moves. A rolling object turns around and around as it moves.

"Sliding and Rolling"—Think About It

1. Complete the sentences to show two ways that sliding and rolling are the same. Put a period at the end of each sentence.

Sliding and rolling objects both move _____

_____

Sliding and rolling objects are both always _____

_____

2. A rolling object does something that a sliding object does not do. What is it?

_____

_____

3. Emma is riding her bike on her driveway. Are the wheels on the bike sliding or rolling? Tell how you know.

_____

_____

_____

4. What surface do the wheels on Emma's bike move across?

_____

_____

5. In hockey, a puck slides across the ice. Kenji found a way to make a puck roll across a floor. How did Kenji make the puck roll?

_____

_____

_____

Things That Spin

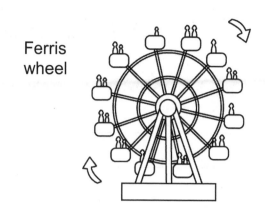

Ferris wheel

Objects spin when they turn around in a circle.

A Ferris wheel is fun because it spins. It turns around and around in a circle. People go high, then low, then high again as the Ferris wheel spins. It is fun to go up high on a Ferris wheel.

Bike

The wheels on a bike spin. Each wheel moves around and around in a circle. When you go fast on a bike, the wheels spin quickly. You cannot go anywhere on a bike if the wheels do not spin.

Merry-go-round

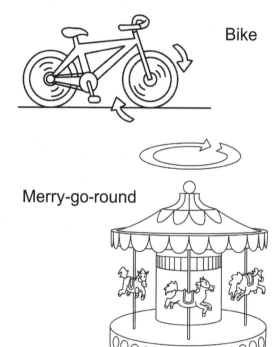

Have you ever been on a merry-go-round? A merry-go-round spins. The horses move around and around in a circle as the merry-go-round spins. The merry-go-round stops spinning when the ride is over.

The **blades** on a fan spin. Turn the fan on and the blades move around and around in a circle. The spinning blades make air move. Then you have a nice breeze to cool you down.

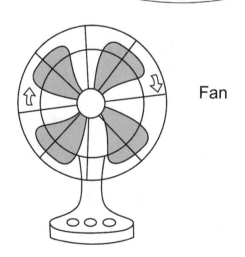

Fan

Can you spin? Yes, you can! First, you need to stand up. Turn your body around in a circle. You can move your feet, but keep them in the same spot on the floor. Do not spin fast and do not turn in a circle too many times. Spinning can make you **dizzy** and you might fall down.

"Things That Spin"—Think About It

1. What is an object doing when it spins?

_____

_____

2. Look at the pictures below. Draw an arrow to each part that spins.

Pinwheel

Hamster exercise wheel

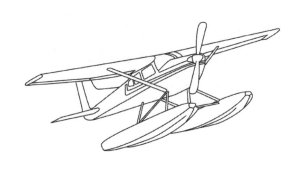

Sea plane

3. What is a breeze? Use clues in the text to help you.

_____

_____

_____

4. How does a fan make a breeze?

_____

_____

_____

5. How can you make sure you do not hurt yourself when you make your body spin?

_____

_____

Things with Wheels

Wheels make heavy things easier to move.

Going on a Trip

How do you take clothes with you when you go away? You can put them in a **suitcase**. A suitcase full of clothes can be heavy. It is hard work to carry a heavy suitcase. Some people have a suitcase with wheels on the bottom. It is easy to pull a suitcase that has wheels.

Wheeled suitcase

Going Shopping

Have you been to a store to shop for food? You can put things you want to buy in a **basket**. A basket is heavy to carry when there are lots of things in it. People use a grocery cart when they want to buy lots of food. A grocery cart has wheels. Pushing a grocery cart is easier than carrying a heavy basket.

Grocery cart

Cleaning the House

Mr. Pinto wants to **vacuum** under his couch. The couch is heavy, but he knows it will be easy to move. The couch has wheels on the bottom. Mr. Pinto pulls the couch away from the wall.

"Look at all that dust!" he says. He turns on the vacuum cleaner. The vacuum cleaner is heavy, but it is easy to move back and forth. Can you guess why?

Vacuum cleaner

"Things with Wheels"—Think About It

1. Why is Mr. Pinto's vacuum cleaner easy to move back and forth?

_____

_____

2. Where in the text can you look to see if your answer for question 1 is correct?

_____

3. Which subheading would you look under to find out about grocery carts?
   Give a reason for your answer.

_____

_____

4. What idea did the author want to explain in this text?

_____

_____

5. Look in the text to find the answers to these riddles.

Riddle 1: You put more and more things inside me as you push me along. What am I?

_____

Riddle 2: You put things inside me. I do not always have wheels, but I am easy to pull when I do. What am I?

_____

Riddle 3: You have to push and pull when you use me. Wheels make me easy to move. I get rid of dust. What am I?

_____

Moving in a Wheelchair

Stella uses a wheelchair to move around.

Moving Forward and Backward

Stella's wheelchair has four wheels. The two wheels at the back are big. Stella uses the big wheels to make the wheelchair move. Wheels are **simple machines** that make things easy to move.

Stella uses her arms to push the big wheels. She pushes the wheels forward to move forward. She pushes the wheels backward to move backward. Stella pushes the wheels harder to make the wheelchair go faster.

Going Around Corners

Stella can make her wheelchair go around corners. She pushes the right wheel harder to turn left. She pushes the left wheel harder to turn right.

Using a Ramp

A wheelchair cannot go up stairs. Many places have a **ramp** for people who use a wheelchair. A ramp is a simple machine. Stella pushes the wheels harder when she goes up a ramp.

Stella does not have to push the wheels to go down a ramp. She holds the railing on the ramp when she goes down. She does not want to go down too quickly.

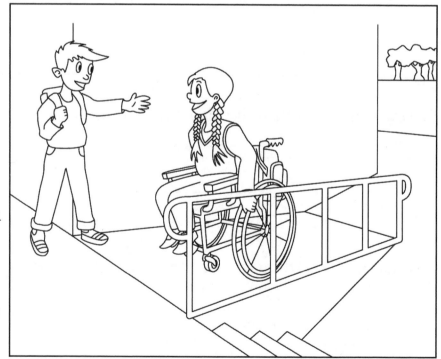

"Moving in a Wheelchair"—Think About It

1. What did the author of the text want to explain?

_____

_____

2. What is the last paragraph about?

_____

_____

3. What part of Stella's body is closest to the small wheels on her wheelchair? Tell how you know.

_____

_____

_____

4. When does Stella push one wheel harder than the other one?

_____

_____

5. Many places with stairs also have a ramp. What is the reason for the ramp?

_____

_____

_____

6. What are two things Stella can do when she pushes both wheels harder?

_____

_____

_____

Be Active Every Day

People need to be active every day. You are active when you do things that make your body move.

Ways to Be Active

There are lots of ways to be **active**. Some people like to play sports. Some people like to play tag or skip with a **skipping rope**. Going for a walk is another way to be active. Everyone can find fun ways to be active. You help your body when you are active.

Helping Your Heart

Your heart pushes blood all through your body. You make your heart work hard when you are active. Your heart gets stronger when you are active every day.

Helping Your Lungs

Your body needs air. You breathe air into your lungs. Your lungs work hard when you are active. You breathe faster when you move quickly. Your lungs work better when you are active every day.

Helping Your Bones

Bones need to be strong. It is easy to break bones that are weak. You help keep your bones strong when you are active every day. You should do something active every day for your whole life. Then your bones will stay strong even when you get old.

There are lots of ways to be active and healthy every day.

"Be Active Every Day"—Think About It

1. What is your body doing when you are active?

_____

_____

2. Why does the text have a picture of a girl riding a bike?

_____

_____

3. The title and the four subheadings in this text are in bold print. What are two ways you can tell the difference between a title and a subheading? (Hint: Think about how they look and where they are.)

_____

_____

_____

_____

4. How does your heart change when you are active every day?

_____

_____

5. How do you know your lungs are working hard when you move quickly?

_____

_____

6. How can you make sure your bones will still be strong when you are old?

_____

_____

7. Create a "Be Active Every Day" poster.

Your Body Needs Water

Lots of things happen in your body. Your brain thinks. Your muscles make you move. Your heart pumps blood. All parts of your body need water to work well.

Your Body Loses Water

The water you drink does not stay inside your body. Water comes out of your skin when you **sweat**. The tears you cry are made of water.

Your body loses water when you go to the bathroom. Your body also loses water in your breath. There is **water vapor** in your breath. You can see the water vapor in your breath on a cold day. The water vapor looks like steam in the air.

Liquids You Drink Contain Water

You do not have to drink water to put water in your body. All liquids you drink have water in them. Drinking water, milk, and juice are healthy ways to put more water in your body. Make sure you drink something six to eight times each day.

Your Body Tells You When You Need Water

Your body has ways to tell you when you need water. You get thirsty. Your skin might feel dry and itchy. You might get **chapped** lips. Chapped lips feel dry and crusty.

Drink plenty of liquids every day for a healthy body.

Drink water and other liquids before you get **thirsty**. Then your body will not have to tell you that you need more water.

"Your Body Needs Water"—Think About It

1. Why does your body need water?

_____

_____

2. Complete each sentence with one or two words from the text.

Water that comes out of your eyes is called _____ .

Water that comes out of your skin is called _____ .

Water in your breath is called _____ .

3. Why does drinking milk or juice put water in your body?

_____

_____

4. How can you tell if your lips are chapped?

_____

_____

Read about Kurt. Then answer the questions below.

Kurt just finished playing soccer. He ran fast. Now he is trying to catch his breath. His face is wet with sweat. Kurt does not feel thirsty.

5. What are three ways that Kurt's body is losing water?

_____

_____

6. Should Kurt drink water? Tell why or why not.

_____

_____

Finding New Friends

Here are some ways to find new friends.

Look for People Who Like Something You Like

Tina loves stickers. She has lots of different stickers. Tina saw that Anna had lots of stickers on her backpack. Tina knew that Anna must like stickers, too. Tina asked Anna if they could trade stickers. Now Tina and Anna are friends.

Look for People Who Are Nice to Others

Jimmy watched Sam at recess. Jimmy saw Sam being nice to people. Sam always let other people take turns. Sam never said **mean** things to people. "I will see if Sam wants to be my friend," said Jimmy. "I think Sam would be a good friend."

Look for Someone Who Needs a Friend

Tony was new in Rachel's class. Tony had moved from another city. He did not know anyone at his new school. Rachel saw that Tony stood by himself at recess. He did not play with others. "Tony needs a friend," said Rachel. Rachel started talking to Tony at recess. They told each other funny jokes. Now Rachel and Tony are friends.

Look for Friends Outside of School

Layla, Tim, and Lee met at Story Time at the public library. They go on Saturday mornings to listen to stories. Layla, Tim, and Lee all go to different schools. They became friends at the public library.

Finding new friends is lots of fun!

"Finding New Friends"—Think About It

1. What did the author of this text want to explain to readers?

_____

_____

2. Which subheading would you look under to read about people who like the same thing?

_____

_____

3. How did Tina know that Anna liked stickers?

_____

_____

4. How did Rachel know that Tony needed a friend?

_____

_____

5. There is one thing that Layla, Tim, and Lee all like. What is it? Tell how you know.

_____

_____

_____

6. Jimmy thinks Sam would be a good friend. How could Jimmy show Sam that he wants to be friends?

_____

_____

_____

"Finding New Friends"—a Letter of Advice

People ask for advice when they have a problem or would like an **opinion** about something. Give some advice to someone about how to find new friends. Explain your thinking to **convince** that person that your advice is the right thing to do.

Dear _____,

_____

_____

_____

_____

_____

_____

_____

_____

_____

_____

_____

Your friend,

_____

Teasing

Teasing is making fun of someone. What happens when someone teases you? Your **feelings** might get **hurt**. You might get **angry**.

Ways People Tease

People can say things to tease you. Tina was running on the playground and she tripped. Pedro said, "Tina is a baby. She does not know how to run yet." Pedro was teasing Tina.

People can do things to tease you. They might laugh at you or make faces. The teacher asked Abdul a question. Abdul said a wrong answer. Linda laughed at Abdul to tease him.

Ways to Stop Teasing

How can you stop someone who is teasing you? Here are some things you can try.

1. Tell the person to stop teasing you. Try not to get angry and yell. Say, "Please stop teasing me. I do not like it."
2. Walk away from the person who is teasing you. Go far away so you cannot hear the teasing.
3. Tell the person how the teasing makes you feel. Some people say, "It hurts my feelings when you tease me." Other people say, "It makes me angry when you tease me."
4. Ask an adult to help you stop the teasing.

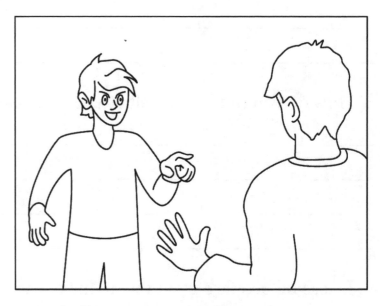

There are ways to try to stop someone from teasing you.

"Teasing"—Think About It

1. What does the word *teasing* mean?

_____

_____

2. Tell two ways people can tease you if they do not use words.

_____

_____

_____

3. How can you tell that this text has two main parts?

_____

_____

4. Which part of the text contains a list?

_____

_____

5. How do you think Tina felt after Pedro teased her? Explain your thinking.

_____

_____

_____

_____

6. Is teasing people a good way to make friends? Tell why or why not.

_____

_____

_____

_____

When You Are Sick

It is not fun to be sick. You might cough or sneeze. You might get a runny nose or have a sore throat. **Germs** got into your body and made you sick. It is important not to spread those germs. The germs could make other people sick, too.

Here are some ways you can stop germs from **spreading** to other people.

Wash Your Hands Often

Germs can get onto your hands. Then the germs can go onto people or things you touch. Wash your hands often so you do not spread germs. Washing your hands gets rid of the germs on them.

Cover Your Mouth When You Cough

A cough sends germs from inside your body into the air. Those germs could make other people sick. Cover your mouth when you cough. That will help to keep germs from spreading.

Do not cover your mouth with your hand when you cough. Germs will get on your hand. You will spread those germs when you touch things. Cover your mouth with the inside of your elbow. You do not touch things with the inside of your elbow, so germs will not spread.

Stay Away from Other People

You might spread germs to people you play with. They might get sick. Try not to get close to other people when you are sick. Tell your friends you will play with them when you are feeling better.

Try not to spread germs when you are sick.

"When You Are Sick"—Think About It

1. What are four ways your body tells you that you might be sick?

_____

_____

_____

_____

2. Why is it important not to spread germs when you are sick?

_____

_____

_____

3. Why is it not good to cover your mouth with your hand when you cough?

_____

_____

_____

_____

4. Why is it important to stay away from friends until you are feeling better?

_____

_____

_____

5. Why did the author write this text?

_____

_____

_____

Birthday Traditions

Your birthday comes on the day you were born. Many people have a special **celebration** on their birthday.

Different **cultures** have different birthday **traditions**. Read about how some children in the United States and Canada celebrate birthdays.

A Birthday Party

Friends and relatives come to a birthday party. Sometimes there are balloons. There might be other **decorations**, too.

Cards and Gifts

People bring cards and gifts for the birthday girl or boy. The gifts are wrapped in colorful paper. It is fun to open the gifts.

A Birthday Cake with Candles

People eat birthday cake at a birthday party. The top of the cake might say Happy Birthday! There are candles on top of the cake.

Two things happen before it is time to eat the cake. First, people sing a song called "Happy Birthday to You." Then the birthday girl or boy blows out the candles on the cake. Now it is time to eat cake!

"Birthday Traditions"—Think About It

1. Your birthday comes on a special day. What happened on this special day?

_____

_____

2. Does everybody celebrate birthdays the same way? Circle Yes or No. Then write the sentence in the text that helped you answer the question.   **Yes   No**

_____

_____

3. Why is each birthday gift a surprise?

_____

_____

4. What happens before the birthday girl or boy blows out the candles on the cake?

_____

_____

5. This text has three subheadings in bold print. Name two other text features in the text.

_____

_____

6. Look in the text to find something special children wear at some birthday parties. Tell what it is and where you found the answer.

_____

_____

_____

A Birthday in Mexico

Pablo lives in Mexico. Read about Pablo's birthday party.

A Sombrero Cake

Pablo's birthday cake is a **sombrero** cake. A sombrero is a Mexican hat. Pablo's cake is shaped like a sombrero. A sombrero birthday cake is a tradition in Mexico.

In Mexico, the birthday boy or girl takes the first bite of cake. There is a special way to do it.

Pablo holds his hands behind his back. He takes a bite out of the whole cake. He does not use a fork or spoon. He bites right into the cake with his mouth. Pablo looks funny with cake all over his face.

Sombrero cake

A Piñata

The best part of Pablo's birthday party is the **piñata** (say it like this: *pin-yah-tah*). The piñata is a tradition at birthday parties in Mexico.

Sometimes the piñata looks like an animal. The piñata hangs from the ceiling. Children take turns trying to break the piñata with a long stick. The children wear a **blindfold** so they cannot see.

Pablo hits the piñata and breaks it. Candies and small toys for all the children come out of the piñata.

Boy with a piñata

"A Birthday in Mexico"—Think About It

1. Why do many children in Mexico have a sombrero cake on their birthday?

_____

_____

2. What does the first picture help you learn?

_____

_____

_____

_____

3. Which subheading would you look under to find out who takes the first bite of birthday cake in Mexico?

_____

4. Pablo takes the first bite of the cake. Then Pablo and all the children laugh. Tell why.

_____

_____

5. What is a blindfold?

_____

_____

6. Does Pablo get to keep all the candies and toys that come out of the piñata? Circle Yes or No. Then write the sentence in the text that helped you answer the question. **Yes No**

_____

_____

Christmas

December 25 is a special day for many people around the world. On this day, many people celebrate Christmas Day.

Christmas Decorations

People start decorating for Christmas when December comes. Many people put up a Christmas tree in their home. They hang colored lights and shiny balls on the tree. Some people put colored lights outside their home or in their windows.

Christmas Traditions

Before Christmas Day, people send Christmas cards to friends and relatives. The cards often say "Merry Christmas."

People sing Christmas songs in December. One Christmas song many people know is called "Jingle Bells."

People give each other gifts at Christmas. The gifts are wrapped in colorful paper. The gifts sit under the Christmas tree until Christmas morning. Then people open the gifts to see what is inside.

On Christmas Day, people eat a special meal called Christmas dinner. Turkey is a favorite food to eat at Christmas dinner. Many people invite friends and relatives to share their Christmas dinner.

Decorated Christmas tree and wrapped gifts

Christmas card

"Christmas"—Think About It

1. Tell three places you might see colored lights at Christmas.

_____

_____

_____

2. How is music a part of Christmas celebrations?

_____

_____

_____

3. What clue in the text shows that Christmas can be a snowy time in some places?

_____

_____

4. What is the date when people open the gifts under the Christmas tree?

_____

5. The text tells two colorful things people see at Christmas. What are these two things?

_____

_____

6. Some people need to put extra chairs at their table for Christmas dinner. Tell why.

_____

_____

_____

Hanukkah

What Is Hanukkah?

Hanukkah is a Jewish celebration that happens every year. Hanukkah starts on a different date each year. Sometimes Hanukkah starts in November, and sometimes it starts in December. Hanukkah lasts for eight days and nights.

Hanukkah is an important celebration for Jewish people around the world.

How Do People Celebrate Hanukkah?

An important part of Hanukkah is the lighting of the Hanukkah **menorah**. The Hanukkah menorah holds one candle in the middle and four candles on each side. The candle in the middle is for lighting the other candles.

People often play a game called **dreidel** (say it like this: *dray-del*). A dreidel is a spinning top with four sides. Each side has a different Hebrew letter on it. Hebrew letters are different from English letters.

People sing special Hanukkah songs. One song is about the dreidel.

There are special foods that many people eat during Hanukkah. One food is potato pancakes. Another food is donuts filled with jam.

People often give each other gifts during Hanukkah.

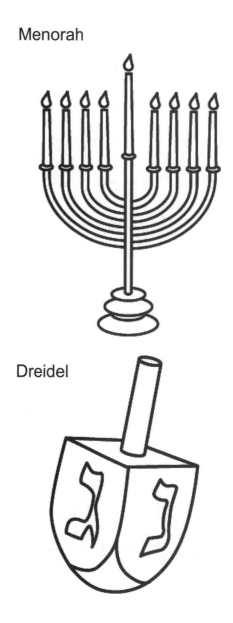

Menorah

Dreidel

"Hanukkah"—Think About It

1. Which sentence tells you that Jewish people celebrate Hanukkah in many different countries?

_____

_____

2. What is the middle candle on a Hanukkah menorah used for?

_____

_____

3. Look at the picture of the Hanukkah menorah. How is the middle candle different from the other candles?

_____

_____

4. How many Hebrew letters are on a dreidel?

_____

_____

5. What special Hanukkah food hides a sweet surprise inside?

_____

_____

6. People sometimes call Hannukah the Jewish Festival of Lights. How is light a part of Hanukkah?

_____

_____

_____

_____

Diwali

What Is Diwali?

Diwali is a festival that started in India. Diwali lasts for five days. Each year, people celebrate Diwali on different dates. Sometimes Diwali is in October, and sometimes it is in November.

Indian families around the world celebrate Diwali.

How Do People Celebrate Diwali?

Many people clean their homes on the first day of Diwali. They believe this will bring them good luck.

Diwali is sometimes called the Indian Festival of Lights. People light **oil lamps** or candles in their home. Some people put strings of lights on the outside of their home.

People wear their best clothes for Diwali. Some people buy new clothes to wear during Diwali.

People give each other small gifts. Many people give each other sweet treats to eat. Some people give candles as gifts.

Diwali can be a loud celebration. Some people light **firecrackers** that make a loud bang. **Fireworks** are also part of Diwali. The fireworks explode with a bang. Then they fill the sky with colorful lights.

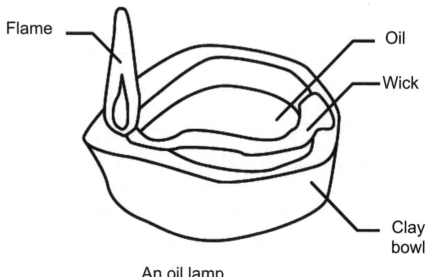

Flame — Oil — Wick — Clay bowl

An oil lamp

"Diwali"—Think About It

1. Who celebrates Diwali?

_____

_____

2. Why do people sometimes call Diwali a Festival of Lights?

_____

_____

3. What three things do people need to make a Diwali oil lamp?

_____

_____

_____

4. Why can Diwali be a noisy celebration? Give two reasons.

_____

_____

_____

5. How do you know that people want to look nice during Diwali?

_____

_____

_____

6. Tell one way Diwali is like another celebration you know.

_____

_____

_____

Eid al-Fitr

Muslim people around the world celebrate Eid al-Fitr (say it like this: *eed al fitter*). Eid al-Fitr is on a different date each year.

Before Eid al-Fitr Comes

People do not eat during daytime for four weeks before Eid al-Fitr. They eat one meal in the morning before the sun comes up. Then they do not eat again until the sun goes down and it is dark. Young children and older people can eat during the daytime.

When Eid al-Fitr comes, people go back to eating during the daytime.

Celebrating Eid al-Fitr

Eid al-Fitr is a happy time. People send cards to friends and relatives to wish them a happy celebration on this day.

On Eid al-Fitr, people dress in their best clothes. Many people hang lights and put up decorations in their home.

Food is an important part of Eid al-Fitr. People make special foods for breakfast. Later in the day, they share a big meal with friends and relatives. Some people eat lamb, fish, or beef at this meal.

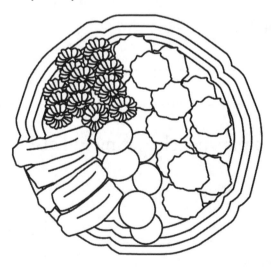

Cookies for Eid al-Fitr

Sweet treats are a favorite part of Eid al-Fitr. Children often get gifts of candy. People eat sweet **desserts** after the big meal.

Eid al-Fitr is also a time to remember that some people do not have enough food and clothes. Families give money to help these people.

"Eid al-Fitr"—Think About It

1. The text does not give a date for Eid al-Fitr. Tell why.

_____

_____

2. In the days before Eid al-Fitr, why do people get up very early to eat their first meal?

_____

_____

_____

3. In the days before Eid al-Fitr, people might look out the window before they eat their second meal of the day. Tell why.

_____

_____

4. How do people make themselves look nice on Eid al-Fitr?

_____

_____

5. Why do people cook lots of food on Eid al-Fitr?

_____

_____

6. Number the following events in the order a person celebrating Eid al-Fitr would do them.

_____ Eat sweet desserts.

_____ Make special foods for breakfast.

_____ Share a big meal with friends and relatives.

The Tricky Turtle

(Based on an African tale)

A farmer went to check his field of corn. He was happy to see the corn growing tall. Then he saw a spot where the corn was not tall. The corn plants were broken and lying on the ground. A turtle was sleeping on the broken corn.

"Turtle, you are in trouble," said the farmer. "Look what you did! I will put you in a pot and make hot turtle soup."

"Yes, cook me if you wish," said the turtle. "But please do not throw me in the river."

"If you are not afraid of fire, I will tie you to a tree," said the farmer.

"Yes, tie me to a tree," said the turtle. "But please do not throw me in the river."

"You are not afraid of rope," said the farmer. "I will put you in a deep hole. You will not be able to crawl out."

"Yes, put me in a hole," said the turtle. "But please, oh please, do not throw me in the river."

"You are not afraid of fire," said the farmer. "You are not afraid of rope, and you are not afraid of a hole. You are only afraid of the river. I will throw you in the river."

The farmer threw the turtle in the river. The turtle swam away. The turtle never went back to sleep in the farmer's field of corn.

"The Tricky Turtle"—Think About it

1. How did the farmer's corn plants get broken?

_____

_____

2. How was the farmer going to make the turtle soup hot?

_____

_____

3. Was the turtle afraid of the river? Tell why or why not.

_____

_____

_____

4. What trick did the turtle play on the farmer?

_____

_____

_____

5. Why did the turtle never go back to the farmer's field of corn?

_____

_____

6. How do you know that this is not a true story?

_____

_____

_____

The Grasshopper and the Ant

(Based on a fable by Aesop)

It was a summer day. Grasshopper was singing. He loved to sing all day long. Ant walked by. She was carrying a big piece of corn.

"That corn is heavy," said Grasshopper. "You look tired. Stop and take a rest. You can sing with me. Singing is fun."

"I have no time to rest," said Ant. "I must **gather** food now. I do not want to be hungry when winter comes. I cannot find food in winter."

"It is summer," said Grasshopper. "Winter is a long time away. You should have fun on a fine summer day."

"I must take this corn to my home," said Ant. "Then I will look for more food. You should look for food, too. What will you eat in winter?"

"I will think about winter later," said Grasshopper. "Today I am having fun singing."

Every day, Grasshopper sang. Every day, Ant carried more food to her home. The days got colder and winter came. Grasshopper got very hungry. He could not find any food. He went to visit Ant.

"Ant, I am hungry," said Grasshopper. "Can you give me some food?"

"No, I cannot," said Ant. "I need my food to last all winter. I worked hard all summer to gather food for winter. You had fun all summer. You did not think of the future, so now you are hungry."

"The Grasshopper and the Ant"—Think About It

1. How does Grasshopper like to have fun?

_____

_____

2. Why does Grasshopper tell Ant to stop and take a rest?

_____

_____

3. Ant does not want to stop and rest. Tell why.

_____

_____

4. Why was Grasshopper hungry when winter came? Give two reasons.

_____

_____

_____

_____

5. Why does Ant tell Grasshopper, "You did not think of the future."

_____

_____

6. This story teaches people a lesson. What is the lesson of the story?

☐ Never give food to a hungry ant.

☐ Look for food when winter comes.

☐ Get what you need for the future.

The Lion and the Mouse

(Based on a fable by Aesop)

On a hot day, Lion lay down in the shade of a big tree. "This is a good place to nap when it is hot," said Lion. He curled up and fell asleep.

Mouse came along and climbed on top of Lion. She ran up and down Lion's back. "This is fun!" said Mouse.

Lion woke up. "Who is tickling my back when I am trying to sleep?" he roared. He put his huge paw on Mouse. "I am going to eat you so you will not wake me up again," said Lion. He opened his mouth wide.

Mouse looked at Lion's big, sharp teeth. "Please do not eat me!" said Mouse. "If you let me go, someday I might be able to help you."

Lion laughed and laughed. "How could a tiny mouse ever help a big lion?" he said. "I will let you go because you made me laugh." He lifted his huge paw and let Mouse go.

The very next day, some hunters caught Lion. They wanted to put Lion in a zoo. The hunters used thick rope to tie Lion to a tree. Then they went to get a wagon to carry Lion to the zoo.

Mouse came along and saw Lion tied to a tree. "What am I going to do?" said Lion. "Some hunters are going to put me in a zoo." Mouse chewed through the thick rope and set Lion free.

"I was wrong," Lion said to Mouse. "You might be tiny, but you have been a big help to me." After that, Lion and Mouse were best friends.

"The Lion and the Mouse"—Think About It

1. Why did Lion want to nap under a big tree?

_____

_____

2. What clue in the story shows that Lion was in a bad mood before he put his paw on Mouse?

_____

_____

3. Why did Lion laugh when Mouse said she might be able to help him someday?

_____

_____

4. Why did the hunters tie Lion to a tree?

_____

_____

5. What was Lion wrong about?

_____

_____

6. This story teaches people a lesson. What is the lesson of the story?

☐ Never try to sleep under a big tree.

☐ A little friend can be a big help.

☐ Always use thick rope to tie up a lion.

The Rooster and the Sun

(Based on a tale from India)

One day, the Sun made the world very hot. It was so hot that people got angry. "Go away, Sun," they shouted. "It is too hot today!"

The Sun got angry when people told him to go away. "I will not shine anymore," said the Sun. He went back to bed and stayed there. He did not rise in the morning. Every day was cold and dark.

Rooster flew to the Sun. Rooster said, "Please get out of bed. Make the world warm and bright again."

The Sun was **stubborn**. He would not change his mind. "I will not get out of bed," he said. "Tell everyone the world will stay cold and dark."

"I will do as you say," said Rooster. "Now I must ask you for a favor. If you stay in bed, I have to fly home in the dark. I am afraid a tiger is waiting to catch me. If I crow, will you come and **rescue** me?"

The Sun said, "You flew a long way to talk to me. Yes, I will rescue you if I hear you crow."

Rooster flew away. Before he got home, he **crowed** as loudly as he could. "Cock-a-doodle-doo!" Then he quickly hid under a bush.

The Sun got out of bed and rose in the sky. He moved across the sky looking for Rooster. The Sun could not find Rooster anywhere.

Every morning, Rooster crows at dawn. The Sun gets out of bed and moves across the sky. The Sun looks for Rooster but never finds him.

"The Rooster and the Sun"—Think About It

1. The Sun stopped rising in the morning. What problem did that cause in the world?

_____

_____

_____

2. This text tells you something that stubborn people do not like to do. What is it?

_____

_____

3. Why does Rooster have to fly home in the dark?

_____

_____

4. What trick does Rooster play on the Sun?

_____

_____

5. What happens in the world when the Sun moves across the sky looking for Rooster?

_____

_____

6. Why does Rooster play the same trick on the Sun every day?

_____

_____

_____

How Communities Change

Communities do not stay the same. Over time, communities change.

People in a Community

The people in a community change. Rosa lived across the street from the house where the Lee family lived. Then the Lee family moved to a different city.

Mr. Goldman moved into the house after the Lee family moved out. Mr. Goldman is a new person in the community. Rosa and her mother said, "Hi, Mr. Goldman. Welcome to our community."

Buildings in a Community

The buildings in a community change. There is a big field behind Carl's house. **Construction workers** are building houses in the field. Now there are new buildings in Carl's community.

A construction worker builds a house in a community.

Sometimes workers tear down an old building in a community. There was an old store near Rosa's house. Workers tore it down.

"Are they going to build a new building where the store was?" Rosa asked her mother.

"No," said Rosa's mother. "They are going to make a park."

"Good," said Rosa. "That will be a nice change in our community."

"Our community is changing all the time," said Rosa's mother.

"How Communities Change"—Think About It

1. What are two things that can change in a community?

_____

_____

2. This text has two subheadings. Why are the subheadings easy to find?

_____

_____

3. Why did the people in Rosa's community change?

_____

_____

_____

4. The text shows one way to be nice to new people in your community. What is it?

_____

_____

5. Workers are changing Carl's community by building new houses. Soon Carl's community will change in another way. How will it change? Tell why.

_____

_____

_____

6. Your school is a community that changes. Give one reason why the people in your school community change from year to year.

_____

_____

People on the Move

How do people go places in a community?

Some people have a car. They drive to places they want to go. There are roads to drive on in the community. People park their cars in driveways, on the side of a street, or in a parking lot. Some people drive a van or a truck instead of a car.

Some people take a bus. Most communities have buses that take people to different places. People wait at a bus stop until the bus comes. They pay when they get on the bus.

People can travel around a community on a bus.

Some people take a **taxi**. A taxi is a car that drives people where they want to go. People call a taxi company. They tell the taxi company where to send a taxi to pick them up. When people get in a taxi, they tell the taxi driver where they are going. People pay the taxi driver at the end of the trip.

Some big cities have a **subway**. A subway has trains that drive in underground **tunnels**. People go to a subway station to get on a train. They pay before they get on the train.

Some people ride bikes. Some communities have special **bike lanes** on some roads. Only bikes can go in bike lanes. Cars and buses cannot drive in bike lanes. Bike lanes keep people on bikes safe.

Some people walk. Many streets have **sidewalks** for people to walk on. Walking on a sidewalk is safer than walking on a street.

"People on the Move"—Think About It

1. What is the main topic of this text?

_____

_____

2. What does a taxi driver do?

_____

_____

3. Can trucks go in bike lanes? Circle the correct answer.   **Yes   No**

Write the sentence from the text that helped you answer the question.

_____

_____

4. Why do bike lanes keep people on bikes safe?

_____

_____

5. What is the second paragraph about? Use one sentence to answer.

_____

_____

6. Jacob and his mom are going to the doctor. They pay at the beginning of the trip. They do not travel underground. How are Jacob and his mom getting to the doctor? Tell how you know.

_____

_____

_____

Hospitals and Community Centers

Many cities have a hospital and a community center.

Hospital

Some people who are sick go to stay in a hospital. There are many rooms in a hospital. The rooms have beds for sick people. A bed is a good place to rest if you are sick.

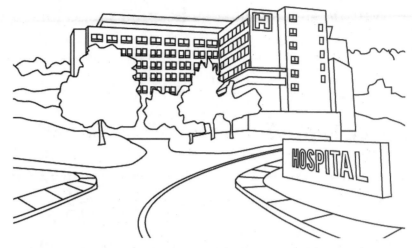

People who are sick might go to a hospital.

Doctors and nurses work at a hospital. They help sick people get better. Many other people work at a hospital, too. **Janitors** keep hospitals clean. Cooks make food for people in the hospital. Some people wash bed sheets. A hospital needs lots of bed sheets.

Community Center

People play sports at many community centers. Some community centers have an indoor rink for skating and hockey. There might be a gym for playing sports such as basketball. Sometimes there is a field where people can play soccer and baseball. There is an indoor pool at some community centers. People swim and take swimming lessons.

Children play soccer at a community center.

Most community centers have rooms where people in **clubs** and groups can meet. Some community centers have clubs for children. The children come together in a room to do lots of fun activities.

"Hospitals and Community Centers"—Think About It

1. Why do sick people in a hospital spend lots of time in bed?

_____

_____

2. Why do you think a hospital needs lots of bed sheets?

_____

_____

3. Read the second paragraph under the bold subheading Hospital. Tell in one sentence what this paragraph is about.

_____

_____

4. What are three places at a community center where people play sports indoors?

_____

_____

_____

5. Jennifer sees a big building. She wants to know if it is a hospital. How can she find out? (Look for a clue in the text.)

_____

_____

6. Does every city have a hospital and a community center? Circle Yes or No. Then write the sentence from the text that helps you answer this question.
Yes   **No**

_____

_____

7. What are the different types of community centers in your community?

_____

_____

_____

_____

_____

8. In your opinion, do community centers make a community a better place to live? Explain.

_____

_____

_____

_____

_____

9. Do you think people would miss having a hospital or community center? Explain.

_____

_____

_____

_____

What Does a School Custodian Do?

Every school needs a custodian. The custodian makes sure that the school is clean, safe, and nice for everyone. Mr. Jones is a school custodian. Read about some of the jobs he does at his school.

All Around the School

Mr. Jones cleans all the floors. He mops and shines the hard floors. He vacuums floors that have carpet. Mr. Jones also keeps the windows clean. He wipes away finger marks on doors and walls.

In winter, Mr. Jones makes sure the school is nice and warm. All year long, he checks for **lightbulbs** that have burned out. He takes out the old lightbulbs and puts in new ones. The students need light to see well.

In Classrooms

Mr. Jones empties the wastebasket. He also empties the pencil sharpener. Once each week, he washes the **chalkboards** and **marker boards**. Then he wipes away any dust he finds in the classroom.

In Hallways

Mr. Jones cleans the drinking fountain and makes sure it works. He wipes up any water on the floor. Someone might slip on a wet floor.

In Restrooms

Mr. Jones cleans sinks, mirrors, and toilets. He checks the toilet paper and paper towels. Then he makes sure that all the toilets flush.

A school custodian changes a lightbulb that has burned out.

"What Does a School Custodian Do?"—Think About It

1. What are two different ways that Mr. Jones cleans floors?

_____

_____

2. Does Mr. Jones clean the gym floor at his school? Tell how you know.

_____

_____

_____

3. Why is checking the lights an important job?

_____

_____

4. What does Mr. Jones use to help him put in a new lightbulb? Tell how you know.

_____

_____

_____

5. What is one job Mr. Jones does to keep people safe? Tell how this job keeps people safe.

_____

_____

_____

6. Your school custodian works very hard to make your school nice for everyone. How could you show the custodian you are thankful?

_____

_____

What Does a School Librarian Do?

Mr. Tanaka is a school librarian. School librarians do many different jobs. Read about some of the jobs a school librarian does.

Helping Students Find Books

A school librarian helps students find books. Paula asked Mr. Tanaka to help her find a picture book. "I like stories about animals," Paula said. Mr. Tanaka showed Paula where to find picture books. He showed her some books with stories about animals.

Making Sure Books Are in the Right Place

A school librarian makes sure all the books are where they belong. Books about different **topics** each have a special place in the library.

Mr. Tanaka saw a book about rocks was on the wrong shelf. He put the book on a shelf with other books about rocks.

School librarians help children find books.

Teaching Students About Books

A school librarian teaches students about books. Today, Mr. Tanaka is teaching students about the **front cover** of a book. "You can find the name of the **author** on the front cover," Mr. Tanaka tells the students.

Choosing New Books

A school librarian chooses new books for the library. "Many students want books about dinosaurs," said Mr. Tanaka. "We have only four books about dinosaurs in the library." Mr. Tanaka is going to get some new books about dinosaurs for the school library.

"What Does a School Librarian Do?"—Think About It

1. What is the main topic of this text?

_____

_____

2. Does this text tell all the jobs a school librarian does? Circle Yes or No. Then write the sentence from the text that helped you answer this question.
Yes   No

_____

_____

3. Mr. Tanaka moved a book about rocks. Where was the right place for the book?

_____

_____

_____

4. Mr. Tanaka is showing students the title page of a book. "The title page of a book tells the title and the author," he says. Which job is Mr. Tanaka doing?

_____

_____

5. Tell two reasons why Mr. Tanaka is getting some new books about dinosaurs for the school library.

_____

_____

_____

What Does a Crossing Guard Do?

Mrs. Hill works as a school crossing guard. Read the questions and answers to find out about her work.

Helping People

Mrs. Hill helps children cross the street safely. She works on a street near the school. Children cross this street when they come to school. They cross the street again when they go home from school.

Mrs. Hill walks into the street. She holds up a sign that says STOP. She blows a whistle. All the cars must stop. Mrs. Hill tells the children when it is safe to cross the street.

Staying Safe

Mrs. Hill wears a **vest** with bright colors. The bright colors make the vest easy to see. Car drivers need to see Mrs. Hill when she is in the **street**. The vest helps keep Mrs. Hill safe.

Time to Work

Mrs. Hill works in the morning before school starts. She also works at lunchtime. Then she works again when school is over for the day.

Mrs. Hill does not work on Saturdays and Sundays. She does not work at all in July and August.

A crossing guard blows her whistle to stop traffic.

"What Does a Crossing Guard Do?"—Think About It

1. Which subheading in the text would you look under to find out about a school crossing guard's vest?

_____

2. What are three things a school crossing guard needs at work?

_____

_____

_____

3. Why is a school crossing guard's vest easy to see?

_____

_____

4. Does Mrs. Hill's vest help keep her arms warm? Circle Yes or No. Then tell how you know.   **Yes   No**

_____

_____

_____

_____

5. Mrs. Hill does not work on Saturdays and Sundays. Tell why.

_____

_____

_____

_____

What Is the Internet?

The Internet is made up of **computers** all around the world. These computers are connected by **telephone lines** or **cables**. The Internet lets computers communicate with one another. A computer that has an Internet **connection** can do two things:

• Send information to other computers that are part of the Internet

• Receive information sent by other computers on the Internet

Not every computer is connected to the Internet. People have to pay money each month to have their computer connected to the Internet.

How Do People Use the Internet?

When people go online, they are connected to the Internet. Here are some different ways people use the Internet:

• To learn information from **web sites**

• To play computer games-

• To share information and photographs with others

• To send and receive **e-mail messages**

• To shop for things

People can use the Internet to send e-mail to friends far away.

Cell Phones and the Internet

Some cell phones can connect to the Internet. That means people can receive and send information over the Internet by using a cell phone instead of a computer.

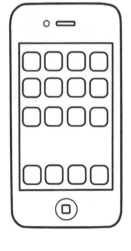

Some cell phones can connect to the Internet.

"What Is the Internet?"—Think About It

1. You have probably used a computer at home or at school to look at web sites on the Internet. Name two topics that you have learned about by looking at Internet web sites.

Topic 1: _____

Topic 2: _____

2. If you have a computer with Internet at home, tell two things you use the Internet to do. If you are not connected to the Internet at home, tell two ways that you would like to use the Internet.

_____

_____

_____

_____

3. List three ways people use the Internet. Use the subheadings to help find the answer.

_____

_____

_____

4. Are there rules or guidelines you have to follow when you use the Internet? Explain.

_____

_____

_____

_____

Convincing People to Buy a Product

Advertising tries to **convince** people to buy the product that is advertised. What are some ways that advertising tries to do this?

Facts about the product

Give Facts About the Product

A **fact** is a piece of information that is always true. Here is an example of a fact: *Space Crunch cereal is made from wheat.* The company that makes this cereal can **prove** that it is always made from wheat. This is a fact because it is always true.

Nick says, "Mmmmm. This is the best cake I have ever had!"

Bakery's Own Cakes—the best you will ever have!

An opinion about the product

Give Opinions About the Product

An **opinion** is a piece of information that is true for some people, but not for everyone. Here is an example of an opinion: *Bakery's Own Cakes is the best I have ever tasted.* Some people might agree that Bakery's Own Cakes is the best cake they have ever tasted. Other people might think that another type of cake tastes better. The opinion that Bakery's Own Cakes tastes best is not true for everyone.

Compare the Product to Similar Products

Imagine that you have created a new cereal called Tasty Bites. You want to convince people to buy your cereal instead of Yummy Crunch. Your advertising could compare Tasty Bites to Yummy Crunch. Here are two examples:

• Tasty Bites has more vitamins than Yummy Crunch.
• Tasty Bites has a toy inside, but Yummy Crunch does not.

Comparing two similar products

"Convincing People to Buy a Product"—Think About It

1. Read the sentences you might see in advertising. Put a check mark beside each sentence to tell whether it is a fact or an opinion.

Statement	Fact or opinion?
a) Super Fast running shoes come in four different colors.	☐ Fact ☐ Opinion
b) You will love your new Super Fast running shoes.	☐ Fact ☐ Opinion
c) Your whole family will enjoy playing the Race to Win board game.	☐ Fact ☐ Opinion
d) Race to Win comes with four game pieces and two dice.	☐ Fact ☐ Opinion

2. What is a fact? Use the text to help find the answer.

_____

_____

_____

3. What is an opinion? Use the text to help find the answer.

_____

_____

_____

4. What is your favorite food? _____

Create a food character. Give it a name. _____

Draw a picture of your food character with your favorite food. Add some words to make an ad.

[drawing box]

5. In what ways does your ad make children want to try your favorite food?

_____

_____

_____

The Wright Brothers

The Wright brothers were Orville and Wilbur. They built and flew the first **plane**. They made the first flight on record in 1903. Over the years, they worked to make better planes. Their work helped others make the planes we see today.

Early Life

Orville and Wilbur read many books. They loved to work on science projects. They made a **printing press**. Then they opened a bike shop. These projects helped them be better **designers**.

They made a heavier-than-air plane. It had a light **engine**. They made the plane so they could control it in the air.

The First Flight

In 1903, they flew their plane at Kitty Hawk, North Carolina. Kitty Hawk had sand dunes so they could land softly. Orville was the pilot. Wilbur ran beside the wing. The first flight took 12 seconds at a speed of 7 miles (11 kilometers) per hour!

Over the years, they made better planes. In 1908, they made their longest flight. It was 2 hours and 19 minutes long.

You can visit the Wright Flyer in the National Air and Space Museum in Washington, D.C.

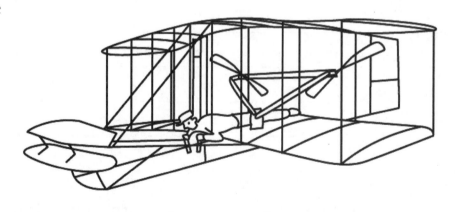

The Wright Flyer had a wood frame covered with fabric. It had an engine, too.

"The Wright Brothers"—Think About It

1. What is the most important event in this text? How do you know?

_____

_____

_____

2. What features in the text help you find information?

_____

_____

_____

3. How does the picture and caption help you understand what you are reading?

_____

_____

4. Why do you think the Wright brothers were able to invent the first plane? What details in the story tell you so?

_____

_____

_____

_____

5. What does the author want you to learn from this text?

_____

_____

_____

_____

Helen Keller

Put your hands over your ears so you cannot hear. Close your eyes as tightly as you can. Imagine living in such a dark world with no **sound**. This was how Helen Keller lived.

Helen Keller

Young Helen

Helen was born in 1880 in Tuscumbia, Alabama. She could see and hear and was very smart.

But when Helen was less than two years old, she had a **high fever**. She was very sick. When she finally got better, Helen was **deaf** and **blind**. She could no longer hear or see.

Breakthrough!

Helen was very upset because she could not talk with people. Her parents found her a teacher named Annie Sullivan. Annie used **sign language** to spell words into Helen's hands. But Helen did not understand.

One day, Annie poured water over Helen's hands. Then Annie spelled W-A-T-E-R into Helen's palm. Suddenly it all made sense to Helen. She learned 30 words that day! From that day, for her whole life, she called Annie "Teacher."

Life with Helen

With Annie's help, Helen liked to swim and hike. She loved animals, especially dogs. Helen wrote books and went to college. She **traveled** around the world. In 1968, Helen died.

Helen showed that people who are deaf and blind can do many things.

"Helen Keller"—Think About It

1. Helen was very brave. Name someone you know who is brave. How does he or she show their bravery?

_____

_____

_____

2. What reason does the author give to explain why Helen Keller became deaf and blind?

_____

_____

3. How old would Helen be if she were alive today?

_____

4. What is the main topic of the paragraphs under the subheading "Breakthrough!"?

   A. Annie and Helen learned how to communicate with each other.

   B. Helen wanted a drink of water.

5. Why do you think Helen liked dogs so much?

_____

_____

6. June 27 is Helen Keller Day. What do you think people can do on that day to celebrate Helen?

_____

_____

_____

Graphic Organizers

Graphic organizers are excellent tools to use for identifying and organizing information from a text into an easy-to-understand visual format. Students will expand their comprehension of a text as they complete the graphic organizers. Use these graphic organizers in addition to the activities in this book or with other texts.

Concept Web – Helps students understand the main idea of a text and how it is supported by key details.

Concept Map – Helps students gain a better understanding of how different subtopics within a text connect to the topic as a whole.

Venn Diagram/Comparison Chart – Helps students focus on the comparison of two items, such as individuals, ideas, events, or pieces of information. Students could compare by looking at which things are the same, or contrast by looking at which things are different.

Fact or Opinion – Helps students to distinguish between statements of fact or opinion. Facts are pieces of information that can be proven to be true. Opinions are pieces of information based on something that someone thinks or believes, but that cannot necessarily be proven to be true.

Cause and Effect – Helps students to recognize and explain relationships between events. The cause is the reason why an event happens and the effect is the event that happens.

Making Connections – Helps students to connect something they have read, or experienced, with the world around them.

Context Clue Chart – Helps students organize clues that the author gives in a text to help define a difficult or unusual word. Encourage students to look for explanations of words within a text.

Drawing Conclusions and Making Inferences Chart – Helps students practice drawing conclusions and making inferences based on their prior knowledge, as well as what they read in the text.

A Concept Web About...

A **main idea** is what the text is mostly about. A **detail** is important information that tells more about the main idea.

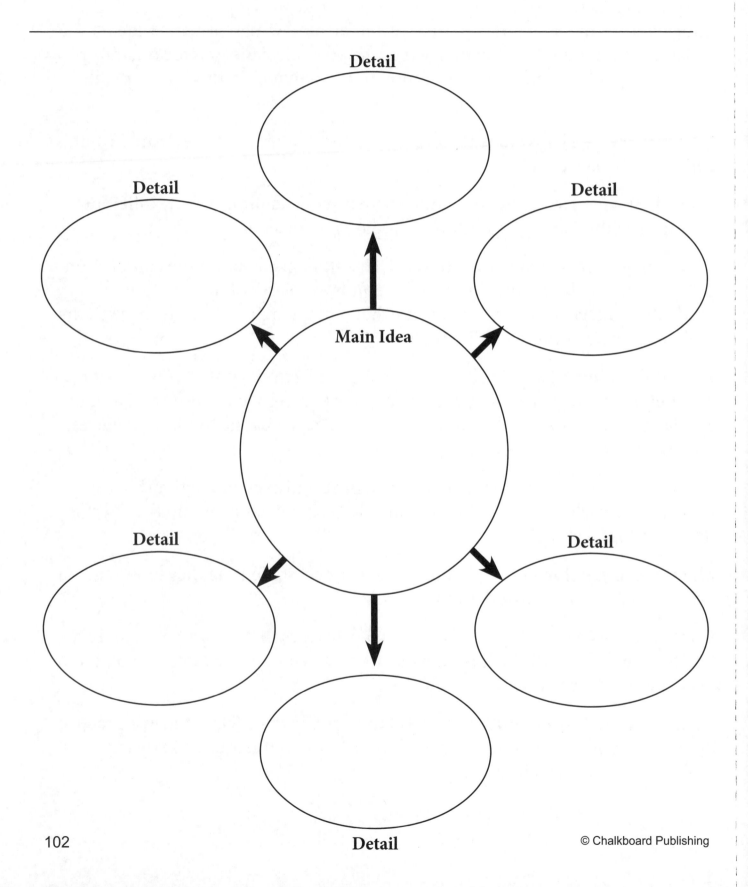

Detail

Detail

Detail

Main Idea

Detail

Detail

Detail

Concept Map

A **main idea** is what the text is mostly about.
A **subheading** is the title given to a part of a text.
A **detail** is important information that tells more about the main idea.

Main Idea

Subheading

Subheading

Subheading

Details

Details

Details

A Venn Diagram About...

_____

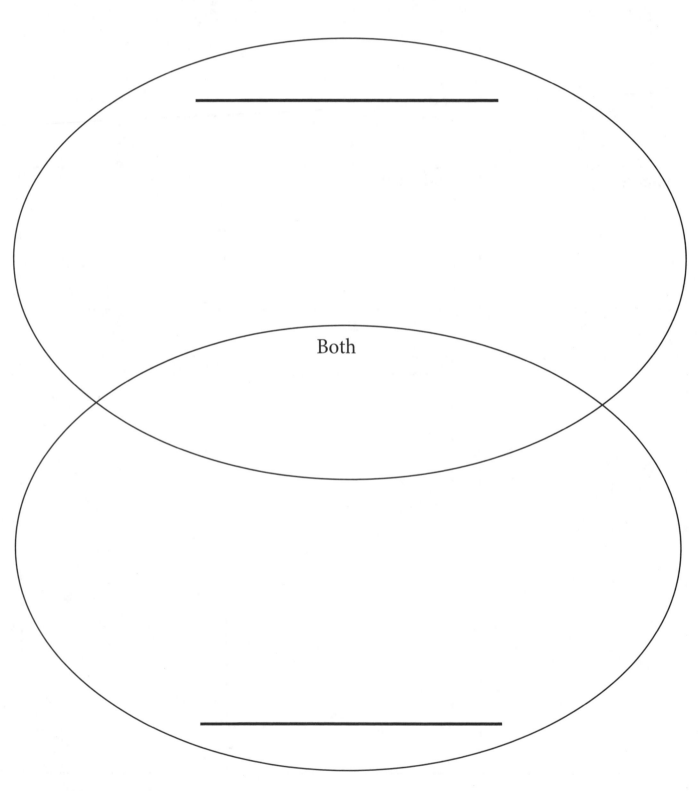

Both

A Comparison Chart

Compared
to

Detailed information

Detailed information

Fact or Opinion

- **Facts** are pieces of information that can be proven to be true.
- **Opinions** are pieces of information based on something a person thinks or believes.

Piece of Information	Fact or Opinion?	How do you know?

Cause and Effect

- The **cause** is the reason something happens.
- The **effect** is what happened.

Cause
Effect

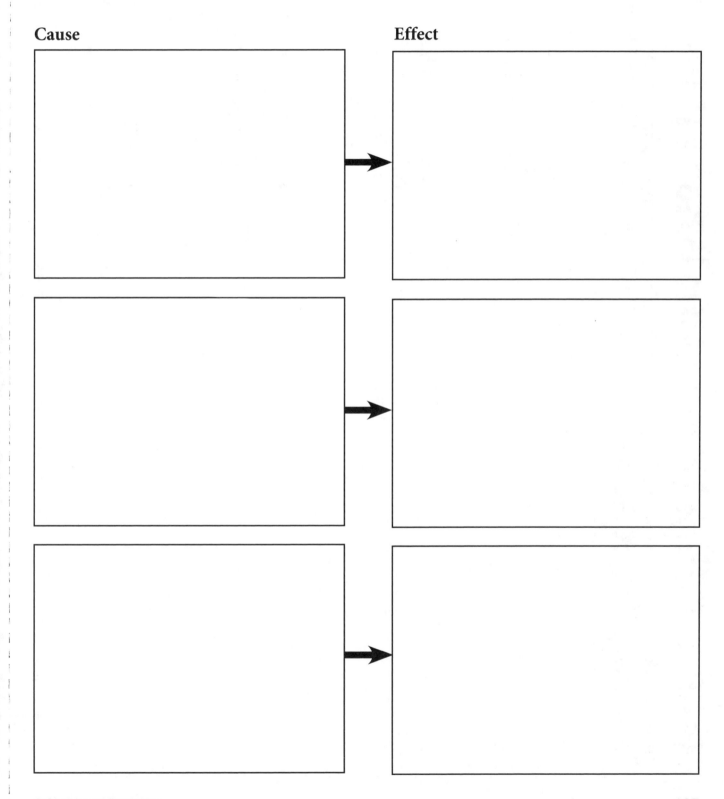

Making Connections with What I Have Read

After reading…	It reminds me of…	This helps me make a connection to…
		☐ something else I have read ☐ myself ☐ the world around me
		☐ something else I have read ☐ myself ☐ the world around me
		☐ something else I have read ☐ myself ☐ the world around me
		☐ something else I have read ☐ myself ☐ the world around me

Context Clue Chart

Context Clues are hints that the author gives in a text that can help you find the meaning of a word.

Word	Context Clue from Text	Meaning of Word

Drawing Conclusions and Making Inferences Chart

We make an **inference** when we combine what we know to be true with new information and come to a conclusion.

What I already know:	Clues from the text I read:	Help me to conclude or infer:

How Am I Doing?

	Completing my work	Using my time wisely	Following directions	Keeping organized
Full speed ahead!	• My work is always complete and done with care. • I added extra details to my work.	• I always get my work done on time.	• I always follow directions.	• My materials are always neatly organized. • I am always prepared and ready to learn.
Keep going!	• My work is complete and done with care. • I added extra details to my work.	• I usually get my work done on time.	• I usually follow directions without reminders.	• I usually can find my materials. • I am usually prepared and ready to learn.
Slow down!	• My work is complete. • I need to check my work.	• I sometimes get my work done on time.	• I sometimes need reminders to follow directions.	• I sometimes need time to find my materials. • I am sometimes prepared and ready to learn.
Stop!	• My work is not complete. • I need to check my work.	• I rarely get my work done on time.	• I need reminders to follow directions.	• I need to organize my materials. • I am rarely prepared and ready to learn.

Reading Comprehension Student Tracking Sheet

Student's Name	Identifies the Purpose of the Text *Student: I can tell you why we read this.*	Demonstrates Understanding of the Text *Student: I can tell you what the text is about.*	Analyzes Text *Student: I can make predictions, interpretations, and conclusions using information from the text.*	Makes Connections to Text (Prior Knowledge) *Student: This reminds me of* • *text-to-text* • *text-to-self* • *text-to-world*	Text Features *Student: I can tell you how different text features help the reader.*

Level 4: Student shows a thorough understanding of all or almost all concepts and consistently gives appropriate and complete explanations independently. No teacher support is needed.

Level 3: Student shows a good understanding of most concepts and usually gives complete or nearly complete explanations. Infrequent teacher support is needed.

Level 2: Student shows a satisfactory understanding of most concepts and sometimes gives appropriate, but incomplete explanations. Teacher support is sometimes needed.

Level 1: Student shows little understanding of concepts and rarely gives complete explanations. Intensive teacher support is needed.

You Are Doing Fantastic!

Keep Up the Wonderful Work!

_____
Name

_____
Date

Answers

A Trip to a Farm, pp. 6–8

1. sheep: Lily and Sandro; Mr. Crane: Sandro; baby pigs: Lily; chicken eggs: Sandro; chicks: Lily and Sandro; corn: Lily; tractor: Sandro
2. The small wheels are at the front of the tractor. The answer is in the diagram.
3. Lily liked holding the baby chick best. Sandro liked sitting on the tractor best.
4. Answers will vary.
5. Answers will vary.

All About Birds, pp. 9–10

1. How are all birds the same?
2. Feathers help keep heat inside a bird's body.
3. Students might respond by saying that people use clothes to help their body stay warm, or they might mention specific articles of clothing, such as coats, jackets, sweaters, etc.
4. My mouth does the same thing as a bird's beak.
5. If an egg gets cold, the baby bird growing inside the egg might die.
6. Encourage students to provide information that is not contained in the text. Students might suggest answers such as the following:
   • An ostrich has black feathers and white feathers.
   • An ostrich has long legs.
   • An ostrich has a long neck.

Dragonflies, pp. 11–12

1. An adult dragonfly has four wings. The answer is in the diagram.
2. Each subheading is a question sentence. Students might point out the use of question words (what, how) at the beginning of each sentence, or the use of question marks at the end of each sentence.
3. Large eyes: A dragonfly uses its large eyes to find an insect to eat.
   Legs: A dragonfly makes a basket shape with its legs and traps the insect inside.
   Mouth: A dragonfly bites the insect it has trapped so the insect does not get away. Then it eats the insect.
4. The nymphs need to crawl up the stem of a plant to get out of the water when they are ready to become an adult dragonfly.
5. An adult dragonfly lays eggs.

Big and Blue, pp. 13–14

1. A baby whale is a newborn whale when it has just come out of its mother's body.
2. Milk from the mother helps a baby blue whale grow quickly.
3. Blowholes and nostrils are both used for breathing.
4. A blue whale is bigger than a dinosaur. A newborn blue whale weighs as much as an adult elephant. An adult blue whale has a body that is as long as three school buses.
5. A blue whale has three fins. The diagram shows there is one large fin on each side and one small fin on top.

Squirrel Adaptations, pp. 15–16

1. Adaptations help all animals survive.
2. The two types of adaptations are body parts and things the animal does.
3. Squirrel Body Parts
4. Student might offer responses such as the following examples:
   • The last paragraph is about squirrels making noises.
   • The last paragraph is about why squirrels make noises.
   • The last paragraph is about squirrels making noises when danger is near.
5. Squirrels can dig up the nuts and eat them when it is hard to find food.
6. A squirrel makes noises to help other squirrels. The noises tell other squirrels that danger is near.

Life Cycle of a Brown Bear, pp. 17–18

1. A den is a cave where a bear hibernates.
2. A brown bear hibernates in winter.
3. The cub's first food is milk from its mother's body.
4. A mother bear teaches her cub how to find food.
5. The cub stays with its mother for two or three years.
6. The four types of text features are title, bold text, subheadings, and illustration.

Life Cycle of a Monarch Butterfly, pp. 19–20

1. Students should indicate the following order:
   4 The caterpillar makes a chrysalis.
   1 A caterpillar comes out of an egg.
   6 The monarch butterfly eats nectar.
   2 The caterpillar eats leaves to grow.
   5 A monarch butterfly comes out of the chrysalis.
   3 The caterpillar sheds its skin as it grows.

2. *Sheds* means "gets rid of."

3. The caterpillars that hatch from the eggs eat milkweed leaves.

4. Students should offer one or both of the following points:
   • The caterpillar grows too big for its skin.
   • The caterpillar has to shed its skin more than once.

5. Students might offer points such as the following:
   • The caterpillar's legs are shorter than the monarch butterfly's legs.
   • The caterpillar has many legs, but the monarch butterfly has only four legs.

Three Types of Ice, pp. 21–22

1. What different types of ice do we see in nature?
2. Paragraph 5
3. Paragraph 4
4. Paragraph 2
5. Paragraph 6
6. Paragraph 3
7. Read the question to see if it is about snow, frost, or hail. Then read the text under the subheading that matches what the question is about.

Freezing Rain, pp. 23–24

1. Very cold air close to the ground makes rain freeze.
2. The second paragraph is about what can happen when freezing rain makes ice on roads.
3. Putting sand on icy sidewalks helps people by making ice less slippery, so people do not slip and fall.
4. Salt makes ice melt.
5. Students could offer one of the following responses:
   • A falling branch can dent a car roof.
   • A falling branch can break the glass on a car.
6. Sand makes ice less slippery. Skaters need slippery ice to skate on.

Fog, pp. 25–26

1. Fog and clouds are both made of tiny drops of water that float in the air.
2. A cloud is high in the sky, and fog is close to the ground.
3. You might not see a car coming. The driver of a car might not be able to see you.
4. They might not be able to see the land, so they will not know where they are.
5. Lighthouses are for helping people in boats. Boats are on a lake or an ocean.

Snow Globes, pp. 27–28

1. The best answer is sphere. If students have not yet learned this word, you might accept answers such as the following:
   • A globe is round.
   • A globe is shaped like a ball.
2. The globe, the base, and the plastic objects inside a snow globe (including the snowflakes) are solids.
3. The globe needs to be hollow so water and plastic objects can go inside.
4. Real snow is made of frozen water. The snow in a snow globe is made of plastic.
5. The snow is at the bottom of the globe before someone shakes the snow globe.
6. Shaking the snow globe makes the water start moving. The moving water pushes on the snowflakes and makes them move around.

How We Use Water at Home, pp. 29–30

1. People, animals/pets, and plants are three living things in the text.
2. People drink water because they are thirsty.
3. Boiling water can hurt you because it is very hot.
4. People use water outside to water plants in their gardens and wash cars.
5. Water helps make dirty dishes clean again.
6. The plants in Hamid's garden got water because it rained.

Wind Makes Things Move, pp. 31–32

1. Wind is air that is moving.
2. Wind makes things move by pushing on them.
3. Wind Makes Trees Move
4. A flag hangs down because there is no wind pushing on the flag to make it fly.
5. The wind will blow the kite away if there is no string to hold.
6. The cloud started moving faster because the wind got stronger.

How Do We Use Air? pp. 33–34

1. The main topic is different ways people use air.
2. You breathe faster when your body needs more air.
3. Frank's tire got flat because it had a hole in it. The tire got flat again because Frank did not cover the hole with a patch.
4. A leaf blower and a hair dryer both blow out air (make air move).
5. A leaf blower blows out air that pushes the leaves and makes them move.
6. Vacuum cleaner

Drying Clothes, pp. 35–36

1. You can squeeze the clothes and see water come out of them.
2. Water turns into water vapor in the air when it evaporates.
3. A clothes dryer blows air on wet clothes. A clothes dryer heats the air it blows on clothes. The warm, moving air dries the clothes quickly.
4. The clothes tumble because the inside of a dryer spins.
5. On a warm, windy day. The air is moving and it is warm, so the clothes will dry fastest on a warm, windy day.

Sliding and Rolling, pp. 37–38

1. Sliding and rolling objects both move across a surface. Sliding and rolling objects are both always touching a surface.
2. A rolling object turns around and around as it moves.
3. The wheels on the bike are rolling. They are turning around and around as they move.
4. The wheels on Emma's bike move across the driveway.
5. Kenji stood the puck up on its side and gave it a push.

Things That Spin, pp. 39–40

1. An object is turning around in a circle when it spins.
2. Students should draw arrows to the top part of the pinwheel, the wheel on the hamster's running wheel, and the propeller on the airplane.
3. Students could offer one of the following responses:
   • A breeze is moving air.
   • A breeze is light wind.
4. The blades on a fan spin and make air move.
5. You can make sure you do not spin fast and do not turn in a circle too many times.

Things with Wheels, pp. 41–42

1. The vacuum cleaner has wheels on the bottom.
2. I can look at the picture of the vacuum cleaner.
3. Going Shopping. People use grocery carts when they go shopping.
4. The author wanted to explain that wheels make heavy things easier to move.
5. Riddle 1: Grocery cart; Riddle 2: Suitcase; Riddle 3: Vacuum cleaner

Moving in a Wheelchair, pp. 43–44

1. Students might offer the following responses:
   • The author wanted to explain how Stella moves around in her wheelchair.
   • The author wanted to explain how Stella makes her wheelchair move.
2. The last paragraph is about how Stella goes down a ramp.
3. Stella's feet are closest to the small wheels. The picture shows this.
4. Students might offer the following responses:
   • Stella pushes one wheel harder when she wants to go around a corner.
   • Stella pushes one wheel harder when she wants to turn right or left.
5. Students might offer the following responses:
   • The reason is that wheelchairs cannot go up or down stairs.
   • The reason is so people in wheelchairs can get to the top of the stairs.
6. Stella can go faster and she can go up a ramp.

Be Active Every Day, pp. 45–47

1. Your body is moving.
2. Riding a bike is a way to be active.
3. A title is always at the top of a page. A title is in bigger print than subheadings.
4. Your heart gets stronger when you are active every day.
5. You breathe faster when you move quickly.
6. You can do something active every day for your whole life.

Your Body Needs Water, pp. 48–49

1. All parts of your body need water to work well.
2. Water that comes out of your eyes is called tears. Water that comes out of your skin is called sweat. Water in your breath is called water vapor.
3. Milk and juice have water in them.
4. Your lips feel dry and crusty.
5. Kurt's body is losing water in his sweat and in his breath.
6. Yes, Kurt should drink water. Students could offer reasons such as the following:
   • Kurt should drink water because his body has lost water.
   • Kurt should drink water before he gets thirsty.

Finding New Friends, pp. 50–52

1. The author wanted to explain ways to find new friends.
2. Look for People Who Like Something You Like
3. Tina saw that Anna had lots of stickers on her backpack.
4. Students might suggest one of the following answers:
   - Tony was new at the school and did not know anyone.
   - Tony stood by himself at recess and did not play with others.
5. Layla, Tim, and Lee all like stories. They went to Story Time at the public library.
6. Accept any reasonable answer. (You might use this question to springboard a discussion about ways students can foster new friendships; for example: waving at and greeting the person when arriving at school; waving and saying goodbye to the person when leaving school for the day; asking the person to be a partner for an activity; offering praise and encouragement during classroom and playground activities; offering help when needed.)

Teasing, pp. 53–54

1. Teasing means making fun of someone.
2. People can laugh at you or make faces.
3. Two groups of words (subheadings) in bold print show that there are two main parts in the text.
4. The second part of the text (Ways to Stop Teasing) contains a list.
5. Students might suggest that Tina felt angry, sad, upset, or had hurt feelings after Pedro teased her.
6. Teasing people is not a good way to make friends. Teasing can hurt people's feelings or make them angry.

When You Are Sick, pp. 55–56

1. You might cough, sneeze, get a runny nose, or have a sore throat.
2. The germs could make other people sick, too.
3. Germs will get on your hands. You will spread those germs when you touch things.
4. You could spread germs to your friends and they might get sick.
5. The author wrote this text to explain how you can stop germs from spreading.

Stay Safe in the Sun, pp. 57–58

1. The author wanted to explain ways to stay safe in the sun.
2. The sun can give you a sunburn. The sun can hurt your eyes.
3. Your skin is red and sore.
4. The pictures with labels show what a brim looks like.
5. Sunshine goes through clouds.
6. Sunglasses are dark so they will let only a little bit of light into your eyes.

Birthday Traditions, pp. 59–60

1. I was born on this day.
2. No. Different cultures have different birthday traditions.
3. The gifts are wrapped in colorful paper.
4. People sing a song called "Happy Birthday to You."
5. Title, picture
6. Children wear hats. The hats are in the picture.

A Birthday in Mexico, pp. 61–62

1. A sombrero birthday cake is a tradition in Mexico.
2. The first picture helps me learn what a sombrero cake looks like.
3. A Sombrero Cake
4. Pablo has cake all over his face.
5. A blindfold is something that covers your eyes.
6. No. Candies and small toys for all the children come out of the piñata.

Christmas, pp. 63–64

1. You might see colored lights on Christmas trees, outside homes, and in windows.
2. People sing Christmas songs in December.
3. The Christmas card shows a snowman.
4. People open gifts under the Christmas tree on December 25.
5. People see colored lights and colorful paper on gifts.
6. Many people invite friends and relatives to share their Christmas dinner.

Hanukkah, pp. 65–66

1. Hanukkah is an important celebration for Jewish people around the world.
2. The middle candle is used to light the other candles.
3. The middle candle is higher than the other candles.
4. There are four Hebrew letters on a dreidel.
5. Donuts filled with jam have a sweet surprise inside.
6. The candles on a Hanukkah menorah give light.

Diwali, pp. 67–68

1. Indian families around the world celebrate Diwali.
2. People light oil lamps or candles in their home. Some people put strings of lights on the outside of their home. (Students might also mention that fireworks fill the sky with colorful lights.)
3. People need a small clay bowl, a wick, and oil to make a Diwali oil lamp.
4. People light firecrackers that make a loud bang. Fireworks explode with a bang.
5. People wear their best clothes or buy new clothes.
6. Students should mention a holiday or celebration that involves a similar custom, such as giving gifts, hanging strings of lights, setting off firecrackers or fireworks, or wearing their best clothes.

Eid al-Fitr, pp. 69–70

1. Eid al-Fitr is on a different date each year.
2. People get up early to eat their first meal before the sun comes up because people don't eat during the day during Eid al-Fitr.
3. People might look out the window to see if the sun has gone down and it is dark.
4. People dress in their best clothes.
5. People cook lots of food so they can share a big meal with friends and relatives.
6. Students should number the events in the following order:
   3 Eat sweet desserts.
   1 Make special foods for breakfast.
   2 Share a big meal with friends and relatives

The Tricky Turtle, pp. 71–72

1. The turtle broke the corn plants by sleeping on them.
2. The farmer was going to put the pot over a fire.
3. No. The turtle was not afraid of the river because the turtle knew how to swim.
4. The turtle pretended it was only afraid of the river so the farmer would throw it in the river. Then the turtle could get away.
5. The turtle knew it could not play the same trick on the farmer a second time.
6. Turtles cannot talk.

The Grasshopper and the Ant, pp. 73–74

1. Grasshopper likes to sing to have fun.
2. Grasshopper tells Ant to take a rest because the corn is heavy and Ant looks tired.
3. Ant wants to gather more food to eat when winter comes.
4. Grasshopper did not gather food in summer. He could not find any food in winter.
5. Grasshopper did not think about what he would eat when winter came.
6. Get what you need for the future.

The Lion and the Mouse, pp. 75–76

1. The shade was a cool place to nap on a hot day.
2. Lion roared when he said, "Who is tickling my back when I am trying to sleep?"
3. Lion laughed because he did not think a tiny mouse could ever help a big lion.
4. The hunters did not want Lion to get away when they went to get a wagon.
5. Lion was wrong that a tiny mouse would not be able to help a big lion.
6. A little friend can be a big help.

The Rooster and the Sun, pp. 77–78

1. Every day was cold and dark.
2. Stubborn people do not like to change their mind.
3. The Sun will not get out of bed to shine in the sky.
4. Rooster crows when no tiger is trying to catch him.
5. The world gets warm and bright.
6. Rooster wants the Sun to get out of bed every day so the world will be warm and bright every day.

How Communities Change, pp. 79–80

1. People and buildings in a community can change.
2. The subheadings are in bold print.
3. The Lee family moved out of a house and Mr. Goldman moved in.
4. You can say, "Welcome to our community."
5. The people will change. New people will move into the new houses.
6. Students might suggest answers such as the following:
   • Some students move away.
   • New students come to the school.
   • Some teachers go to teach at a different school.
   • New teachers come to teach at the school

People on the Move, pp. 81–82

1. The main topic is how people go places in a community.
2. Students might suggest one of the following answers:
   • A taxi driver drives a taxi.
   • A taxi driver drives people where they want to go.
3. No. Only bikes can go in bike lanes.
4. Cars and buses (and other vehicles) cannot drive in bike lanes. People on bikes will not get hit by a car or bus.

5. The second paragraph is about taking a bus.
6. They are taking a bus. They pay at the beginning of the trip, so they are not taking a taxi. They do not travel underground, so they are not taking a subway.

Hospitals and Community Centers, pp. 83–85

1. A bed is a good place for sick people to rest.
2. There are many rooms with beds in a hospital.
3. Students might offer one of the following responses:
   • This paragraph is about jobs in a hospital.
   • This paragraph is about people who work in a hospital.
   • This paragraph is about what people who work in a hospital do.
4. People play sports indoors at an indoor rink, in a gym, and in an indoor swimming pool.
5. Jennifer can look for a sign that says "Hospital."
6. No. Many cities have a hospital and a community center.
7. Answers will vary. Sample answers: indoor pool, gym, indoor running track, hockey arena, skating rink, football or soccer field, baseball diamond, basketball court, tennis court, seniors' center
8. Answers will vary. Sample answers: Community centers bring people together to have fun and to learn. People can meet friends and make new friends there. Community centers also give people something fun to do.
9. Answers will vary. Sample answers: Yes, I think people would miss having a hospital or community center. Having a hospital close by is good when there is an emergency or when you want to visit someone who is in the hospital. If there was no hospital, people would have to travel farther to find one. Having a community center close by gives people something to do that they can get to easily. It also gives them a place to meet friends or make new friends. If there was no community center, people would have fewer places to have fun and meet friends.

What Does a School Custodian Do? pp. 86–87

1. Mr. Jones mops and shines hard floors. He vacuums floors that have carpets.
2. Yes. The text says that Mr. Jones cleans all the floors. (Students might also point out that cleaning floors is described under the subheading All Around the School.)
3. Students will not have enough light to see well if some lightbulbs are burned out.

4. Mr. Jones uses a ladder. The picture shows him using a ladder.
5. Mr. Jones wipes up water on the floor so people do not slip.
6. Students might suggest ideas such as the following:
   • Express their thanks to the custodian when they see him or her around the school.
   • Make an individual or class card for the custodian.
   • Make a class poster expressing their thanks and display it in the classroom or hallway.

What Does a School Librarian Do? pp. 88–89

1. The main topic of the text is jobs a school librarian does.
2. No. Read about some of the jobs a school librarian does.
3. The right place for the book was on a shelf with other books about rocks.
4. Mr. Tanaka is teaching students about books.
5. Many students want books about dinosaurs. There are only four books about dinosaurs in the library.

What Does a Crossing Guard Do? pp. 90–91

1. Staying safe.
2. A school crossing guard needs a stop sign, a whistle, and a vest.
3. The vest is easy to see because it has bright colors.
4. No. The picture shows that the vest does not have sleeves.
5. Children do not go to school on Saturdays and Sundays.

What Is the Internet? pp. 92–93

1. Ensure that students have chosen two different topics.
2. Students might offer that they use the Internet to send and receive e-mails, use instant messaging to chat with friends and relatives, find information for projects, and to learn about something they are interested in.
3. Students should list any three of the following answers:
   • to learn information from websites
   • to play computer games
   • to share information and photographs with others
   • to send and receive e-mail messages
   • to shop for things
4. Answers will vary. Sample answer: I can be on the Internet only a certain amount of time. I need to have adult supervision.

Convincing People to Buy a Product, pp. 94–96

1. a) Fact, b) Opinion, c) Opinion, d) Fact
2. A fact is a piece of information that is always true.
3. An opinion is a piece of information that is true for some people, but not for everyone.
4. Ensure that students have drawn a food ad.
5. Ensure that students support their answer.

The Wright Brothers, pp. 97–98

1. The Wright brothers flew their plane in Kitty Hawk, North Carolina in 1903. It was the first recorded flight ever.
2. captions, bold print, subheadings
3. Example: They help me understand what the plane looked like. It had two wings made of wood and covered with fabric.
4. Example: They were curious. The story says they read a lot and did many science projects.
5. Example: how the first heavier-than-air plane was invented

Helen Keller, pp. 99–100

1. People show bravery by living with tough situations. Brave people help people in need, even if there is danger. Some people show courage by living with painful illness. Other people show bravery by doing things that scare them, such as giving a speech, talking to a bully, or standing up for a friend.
2. When Helen was less than two years old, she had a high fever. She was very sick. When she finally got better, Helen was deaf and blind.
3. Helen was born in 1880 so if she were alive today, she would be more than 130 years old.
4. A. Annie and Helen learned how to communicate with each other.
5. Students may say that Helen might have liked dogs because she could touch their soft fur, smell them, and she liked it when dogs licked her face. She could feel them moving around her.
6. On Helen Keller Day, people can read about Helen and watch movies or plays about her. They can learn sign language and find out about other ways to communicate with disabled people. They can spend time with disabled people and find out about the many things they are able to do.